Rackhouse Publishing Inc. & Culture Lounge Jax Present

TEN TOES DOWN

Volume 2

Rackhouse Publishing

Read to Learn. Write to Remember

ISBN-13: 978-1-7371987-9-6

For information about custom editions, special sales, premium and bulk purchases, please contact:
Rackhouse Publishing
Rackhousepublishing@mail.com

First Edition

Printed in the U.S.A

Contents

DEFINING MOMENTS: PAST, FUTURE, PRESENT
Written by Love Reigns

Within this moment
there is opportunity to redefine an existence
a resilience you had no idea you were properly suited for
Armor scraped up and dented
Remember when you wanted to give up?
Thought that you would never live up to the dreams of who you were
told you were supposed to be
So living authentically was kind of never your thing
A caged bird just waiting for the opportunity to sing or to find
somebody with the lyrics
waiting for the ultimate composer to lead you to the right note but
instead you choked on the thought of lifting your voice beyond those
bars constructed with your own hands
wondering how many more seeds you gotta plant before you can finally
see the bloom
the fulfilling fruit of your labor
You savor doubt like it's laid out and filleted on a plate in front of you
You hesitantly chew
Because you know that there is something more
You feel it
You saw it with your third eye when it was once pointed out
That who you were then was only a portion of the clay to help mold you
into who you will be tomorrow
The one who will strategically borrow those life lessons
And reshape them into blessings
Dressing up in your armor like a badge of honor
You'll wear scars
That not only show all that you've been through
But hold remnants of the concrete you broke through
You beautiful rose, you
Quotin Pac like a score to your life
"And if you fall, stand tall and comeback for more"
For every dream you poured into
You'll begin to see every vision come to fruition
Your life is the ultimate mission
The true purpose fulfilled
Keep pushing
And keep raising the bar for no one else but you
Push through
Through the tears and the doubt
This is the only moment you have
Make it count

Introduction

Melynda Rackley, Rackhouse Publishing Inc. CEO

I have read many books in my life and worked with some amazing authors along the way. The one thing they have all had in common was a changed mind and a defining moment that compelled them to share their stories. I can honestly say, this *Ten Toes Down* series has been one of my favorites! In volume one, seven authors dug deep to share knowledge on the mindset for greatness through stories of humility, grit and integrity. In this edition, twelve authors share their defining moments with purpose, change, growth and courage. Each contributing author fearlessly pulls back the veil and gives an unfiltered glance at the growing pains that come with the defining moment. As they share individual wisdom nuggets for finding joy in pursuing purpose, they stand united by their paths. From entrepreneurship to love and everything in between, the precious gems in this volume take it to a different level altogether.

As a stroke overcomer, mother, podcast host and publisher I know all too well how easy it is to feel overwhelmed with life and run away from the things that make you sweat. I know what it's like to start over time and time again and how it feels to finally succeed. Both winning and losing require us to dig deep and stand ten toes down for the purpose, vision or dream to be fulfilled. It's only then we are able to see the beauty in a moment and redesign the path for success. Defining moments often happen after we are done with all of the planning and right in the middle of a purposeful pursuit. As a result of these experiences, we learn from our

i

struggles and find the courage to change.

This book is carefully crafted to stir you to take a closer look at your own defining moment, so you can stand ten toes down and go after your purpose!

I

PURPOSE

"Sometimes you've got to let everything go – purge yourself. If you are unhappy with anything...whatever is bringing you down, get rid of it. Because you'll find that when you're free, your true creativity, your true self comes out."

~TINA TURNER

1

A SPOONFUL OF PURPOSE

"Never be limited by other people's limited imaginations."
—Dr. Mae Jemison, first African-American female astronaut

TIERRA EDWARDS

DEDICATION

I dedicate this chapter to PURPOSE. I also dedicate this chapter to God for the gift of creativity, imagination, words, and insight. To my parents and to the lineage of women who came before me. Thank you all for everything you have imparted into me.

I also dedicate this chapter to the seeds of purpose that will be sown. May they grow abundantly.
Love, Tierra.

"It is my prayer that I move from mundane to intentional living. That I ultimately Pop! (Pursuit of Purpose). That my gifts I have been given in this lifetime are used to their max, that I tap into my highest potential."

It's important that I start this chapter here. The year 2015 was one of the first monumental years of my life filled with unexpected occurrences, lessons on life, and obstacles to overcome. February 23rd, 2015, I was officially divorced. Any extra activities (choir, greeter, fifth grade bible schoolteacher, specialist at the local pregnancy resource center, book club leader for girls) I was a part of leading up to the separation and divorce, I had stopped. I was worn out, felt like a failure, and totally blind sighted.

I was familiar with divorce because it was a regular occurrence in my family. Divorce was the last thing I ever wanted to become a part of my own story, let alone a divorce ending because of physical abuse. The divorce and all the moments preceding led me to one of the darkest moments of my life. It was very hard for me to focus, I cried daily; there was even a moment when I sat on the floor with my back against the bed with so little self-worth that I contemplated what it would be like to inflict pain onto my body that would be exceedingly greater than the pain I was feeling in my heart. There were even nights I contemplated retaliating against my husband at the time because of the anger and resentment that had built up inside. Needless to say, no harm was done, I valued my life much more than that. Thank God! My family and friends hated what I was going through. I remember my mom coming over to visit during that time and as soon as she walked in the door and sat down she began to cry. Although she would not respond to me when I asked her what was wrong, it was clear she was reliving her own pain as she watched me go through this divorce. I honestly did not know how to emotionally handle what I was going through in that season and was way over my head.

My purpose of one day making it my life mission to pour into girls and women was about the only thing that kept me going. I knew this season, amongst many others, was equipping me with what I needed to fulfill my purpose. I must say that season was one of the hardest seasons to show up for. I was in the middle of earning my culinary degree (which I almost dropped down to a certificate) and working full time as an orthodontist assistant (so I was averaging around three or four hours of sleep at night). I managed to put my big girl panties on and graduated with perfect attendance and an Associates Degree. Pushing forward in that season gave me an experience to look back on that will always remind me of what I am capable of, and there is nothing too big that I can't overcome! I look back on that season as often as I need the reminder.

Although the original picture I painted for my life looked a lot different now. I originally had plans of not only a successful marriage but kids that would soon follow, a spouse that would be there along the way for moral support as I pursued my culinary career. However, I had a whole new canvas in front of me waiting to be painted. This canvas was clear, bright, and mine to paint.

The journey continued. Fast forward to 2017, I was in a brand new apartment and still working as an orthodontist assistant instead of using my new culinary degree. There were lots of new changes. Here I made a conscious decision to start implementing a minimalistic routine into my life. I first started with going through every single room in my home and clearing things out that I didn't need, wasn't using, or had too much of.

Secondly, I decided to take the internet out of my home. The main usage at the time was to stream services such as Netflix, Hulu, and Firestick. The television was later removed as well. Thirdly, I jumped out of a twelve year career as an orthodontist assistant that no longer served a purpose outside of a flow of income.

In 2018 I downsized, moved out of my apartment and experienced my dream of RV living for a few months. My desire for a minimalist lifestyle approach was the motion behind this change. I no longer desired to live paycheck to paycheck, nor spend half of my income on rent alone. I ultimately wanted a little more freedom in life and was tired of being weighed down by things that didn't hold a high priority in my standards and value of living. The RV living experience was short lived. In the process of making these changes, my role as a consumer was reshaped, I was less accustomed to holding onto things, I experienced a genuine sense of what I really need to be happy and I managed to save my first $1,000! Although I didn't get to stay in the RV as long as planned, and that did put me in an unexpected situation to quickly find a Plan B, if I had to do it all over again, I would!

I later found a room to rent in a wonderful home with a Nigerian family, whom I cultivated a long lasting relationship with. This home was full of love, family, culture, and faith. It was in that environment that I began to have more dialog with God. This was a pivotal moment because this was the first time since my divorce that I had the desire to consistently speak to God.

Like many, I had my first real test of faith. I found myself completely cutting out all things God, because of the disappointment I experienced within the marriage. The disappointment of specifically preparing myself for marriage (which included four years of abstinence and intentional living), only to marry someone who would end up physically abusing me, and feeling like I heard wrong from God. I needed to speak with God to seek understanding, how to forgive, and obtain a lighter heart, but I really didn't know how to. I needed to pray, but because all of my prayers seemed to go unanswered and I ended up with a divorce, I honestly didn't have a desire to. I also needed to write in my journal so I could release everything that was building up inside of me and sort through, but I found it too hard to. Although I knew everything happens for a reason, and there isn't anything God wouldn't use for his purpose, I eventually realized people failed, but God didn't. I received that revelation and found comfort by being encouraged by my church family and meditating on the scriptures: Genesis 50:20 and Ecclesiastes 3:1-11. But the lines of communication still needed to be reestablished between God and I. Not to mention my zeal for life needed more resuscitation; and that time had come.

During this time I began to desire more out of life. Although I'd jumped out of my long time career as an orthodontist assistant and downsized my living quarters, so that I didn't necessarily have to live to work, there was still a staleness that lingered there. There was still something more at the end of the day, something else I desired. I began to realize I hadn't quite produced certain things out of life because of the context of which I had been trying to produce them. Up until that point I'd experienced living life from my shadow.

Although I had accomplishments I was proud of, like my degree, there was still much more I was supposed to be doing. Yes, I had obtained a Culinary Degree and was working in the field, but there was still more I wanted to do and create with my degree. But the question was how would I get there? When would I get there? Who did I need to become to reach that point?

So one day while writing in my journal I began to write out I AM affirmations that affirmed who I wanted to be. Afterwards I started elaborating what it would be like for me to become those things. They say you have to get specific to get specific results. I wrote what those qualities and characteristics meant to me and how they would look played out in my life.

Those characteristics were:

1. Decisiveness, that meant making quick decisions to cut out procrastination.

2.Discipline, that meant for me to stick with goals I set out to do no matter what!

3. Minimalist, that meant continuing to consume less, remain unattached from "things"'.

4. Vegetarian, set out on a journey to be as plant based as possible to feel and be as healthy as possible.

5. Lover, always choose to love and release anything outside of that from my heat

6. Chef, continue on my culinary path.

7. Naturalist, honor the natural ways of living as much as possible

8. Destiny Seeker, and Risk Taker, meaning don't be afraid to take risks. And do it scared if I had to! No Risk, No Reward!

I got a pink sticky note shortly after and with a black sharpie I wrote those characteristics down and placed the stickies onto the dashboard of my car, right by the radio volume controller. This paragraph surely begins to work as you read more into the chapter, and I use these traits to this day.

At the time I was working as a cook in an Indian Restaurant and doing independent contract work as a Personal shopper, which I would eventually start doing full-time. The sticky notes in my car served as a reminder to me everyday of what I wanted to possess, and because I spent so much time in my car, that was the perfect place for those reminders to be placed. I began to align my thoughts and actions with those characteristics. You may be asking how exactly did I start the alignment process? I basically used that to determine all of my actions, thoughts, and decisions. For example Vegetarian was one of the characteristics, so that meant everything I even thought about buying and bought needed to reflect this. Decisiveness was another big one on the list, so every time I was in a decision making moment I needed to be exercising my ability to make quick sound decisions, and ultimately trusting myself. I pretty much carried that list in my head with me and it was my rule of thumb.

Also on my list was a Chef, Destiny Seeker, and a Risk Taker. I had a whole culinary degree and gift to put to use, I wanted to start exploring my capabilities and really pushing myself so I set out to officially launch my Chef services to the world! Although I knew it wasn't quite in alignment with my ultimate goal and the reason I went to culinary school, it was where my head was at the time and what I felt was right. This plan was definitely one for the books! I had this elaborate plan to invite friends, family, local culinary influencers and really put myself out there and out of my shadow! I was also open to moving away from home as well, so I put in a few resumes that were in different states. To my surprise, but definitely not to God's, I ended up receiving a call from one of the chefs requesting that I come down for an interview. The location of this interview was right off the coast of Georgia! I remember being absolutely floored that the call was happening and this was an opportunity.

I sent the resume off, yes, but I really didn't think anything of it. I gave the opportunity a thought and responded with a yes and set a date to drive five hours away from home, booked an Airbnb and prepared myself to do my first ever cooking interview! I was all kinds of nervous but I was aligning my actions and thoughts with the characteristics of being Decisive, Chef, Destiny Seeker, and a Risk Taker. This was an opportunity given to me by destiny, and the seeker and risk taker in me jumped on it. I wanted to experience everything that moment had to offer me no matter the outcome.

Needless to say I faced my fears, took on a risk (not really), made a decisive decision, drove five hours, cooked three entrees, passed the interview and was offered the position before I left that day! Driving home that evening to Atlanta was a complete high, I was on top of the clouds. Over the days following the interview, I began to prepare for this move that would happen in a little under a month. As the days rolled on everything fell into place and it became apparent that this direction and move was just for me and my purpose. I found an apartment to move into down there, saved up the necessary money to move, including donations from family and friends who were just as excited about this journey as I was. The days leading up to the move were very exciting and I was confident!

March 18th, 2019 was the start of an amazing journey where I was taken from the familiar and immersed into the unknown. Everything began to fall into place from finances, who would help me move, where would I live in less than a month's time! This moving process was so smooth and completely working itself out! I just had to show up. And because the preparation went so smoothly, I knew there was only one reason why. God. I began to see through everything unfolding before my eyes and our conversations that he wanted me down on that coast. God wanted him and I together again. Alone. He wanted to finish what he'd started. Each day I rose, and my vision became clearer. I knew I was here for a purpose and I had to receive everything this moment had for me. Life felt like a vacation for me everyday.

When I wasn't at work I was on the beach. I had always dreamed of the beach being right at my fingertips. And it was. After about six months working at my new job, I began to feel another nudge. In some ways, I felt like a hamster on a wheel going round and round with no direction. I realized that nudging was Purpose knocking at my door.

That nudge was a call to do and be more. A call to step out of the shadows more. A call to share more of my gifts to the world. It was in that season *Born4Purpose* was born. It started as a platform I created on social media to encourage others to live more purpose filled lives and to ultimately live beyond existing. The organization was created out of a place where purpose resides. A place inside of me. A place that eagerly wants to share the lifeline of purpose. *Born4Purpose* is my purpose. My purpose is to share the gift of purpose, and plant seeds of purpose in others. I believe it's one of the greatest gifts each one of us is given. I believe it's what makes the world go round. Imagine a world where everyone is operating with intentionality, gifts and placing their authentic piece to the puzzle! That's a powerful world and that is what I envision.

Born4Purpose isn't just a community but it represents my highest self, my gifts, and more powerfully it represents coming out of my shadow! Although my shadow has always been present, I never knew what my shadow consisted of until I signed up for an online inner child workshop and shadow work class. As I began tapping more into purpose and living, the parts of me that were hiding started to come out. I also began to receive healing fully from my divorce. The more I learned about myself, the more I began to see the parts of me that allowed me to choose certain men and entertain certain relationships including my husband due to my emotional immaturity and rejection wounds that stemmed from my childhood. You can only heal and grow from the things that you are aware of. Many look for healing power outside of themselves and they think if someone else can do x, y, z I will feel better. But the reality is it all starts with yourself. I began to pick myself up off the floor and the healing gave me power and control over my life. My time in solitude away from my hometown was starting to transform me, in ways I did not imagine. My inner light began to shine more and more bright.

For the first time in thirty five years I knew what wounds I had and what my triggers were, and not feeling accepted was a big one. I overlooked a lot of red flags, overcompensated, didn't set boundaries, and chose poorly romantically, and didn't go after my dreams fully because of unhealed wounds. I received a brand new perspective and a lighter heart. I began to learn more about what it looked like to be present, be me, and shine. I established more of a voice by setting boundaries in my relationships and vocalizing when one was crossed; for example if something didn't feel right that was said or done, I made sure to one listen to myself and two vocalize the feeling/thoughts no matter how uncomfortable it made me feel, and lastly give consequences by holding people accountable without fear. Also eliminating overcompensating by living in the truth of my worth, and not rejection by putting me first and only giving from a cup that I first drank from. I also started to record in depth video content on my social media platform. Recording myself sharing personal accounts and stories of my life amongst other things was something I'd never done before, but I knew it was what God was calling me to do because of the insurmountable joy I received while doing it and the impact I was creating in others lives. I began to elevate the parts of me that had never been seen. As things came to the light, I could finally heal them. And as those things were healed they were seen in their proper light.

Everyday I created a piece of content for *Born4Purpose* I sowed seeds into the world, which in turn sowed seeds into myself. I grew roots, shed old leaves and grew new flowers. Establishing *Born4Purpose* was a silent contract I had made to myself to discover and live the *why?* in which I was born.

Born4Purpose is dedicated to the season of my life where I was divorced. It's a movement dedicated to awakening purpose. It's a movement for the young girl who is trying to find her way and doesn't feel she belongs. For the junior in high school who is trying to find the path best suited for her once she graduates. For the young girl whose innocence has been snatched. The girl who has life growing in her belly and is contemplating abortion. For the woman who is in the midst of a marriage that doesn't edify her, or after a divorce and she has lost herself. To the woman in prison who has given her purpose a death sentence. The woman in the homeless shelter who doesn't know how she got there. The woman in the battered shelter who has equated her worth to the number of times she has been hit.

It's my mission to awaken and to plant seeds of purpose where it's never been discovered or simply lost. It's my purpose for girls and women to identify with who they are, what gifts are inside them, and all they have to offer the world! *Born4Purpose* believes there is no life or life circumstances by coincidence, but for purpose. I understand there are plenty of things that get thrown into our life's path, but those things weren't meant to stop anything. They were allowed just for us to use on our journey to purpose. A few days before I had my initial meeting to begin publishing *"Spoonful of Purpose: Guided Journal"*, which would also grant me the opportunity to be writing the chapter that you are currently reading in *Ten Toes Down: Volume 2.*

I had some words that seemed to signify death. I had shared my vision and plans to publish my journal with someone who is very close to me, someone you would expect to give you the best wishes and encouragement. Unfortunately, but fortunately the words I heard were, "I don't think you will be able to publish anything, it's too hard, and it takes a lot of work. If you can get something published, I will be very surprised, but I don't think you will be able to do it."

Time froze and my heart stopped when I heard those words. Those words didn't stop me though. As a result of the healing I had done, and most importantly, because of the purpose I knew I was sent here for, they didn't hurt as bad. My mission was much bigger than someone's perceptions or thoughts. It is my belief (Jeremiah 1:5) that God not only knew us before we were placed into our mother's womb, but he gave us a purpose too. And it is those seeds that I have come to sow and I have just sewed inside you. Make sure to water your seed, and watch it grow.

Before I formed you in the womb I knew you, before you were born I set you apart;
-Jeremiah 1:5 NIV

"I understand
there are plenty of
things that get
thrown into our
life's path, but
those things
weren't meant to
stop anything.
They were allowed
just for us to use
on our journey to
purpose."

TIERRA EDWARDS

2

BREAK THE GLASS & RAISE THE BAR!

"The cost of liberty is less than the price
of repression."
—W.E.B. Du Bois

DESTINY WHITEHEAD

DEDICATION

I dedicate my chapter to my children Jordyn and Virgo. You both have inspired me to go harder than I normally would. Thank you for being my biggest supporters. You've taught me patience and understanding on a level that is unfathomable. I love you both more than life.

After working in a corporate environment for thirteen years and my entire adult life, it was time for me to sever ties. I'm the oldest out of my other two sisters. We grew up in a semi-strict two parent home. I've always had the guidance of my mom and dad to help fuel some of my decisions. They didn't play about certain things and being lazy was one of them.

Growing up, I witnessed my mother go on deployment with the Navy over and over again. This is where I believe I got my work ethic from. Although I would be a little sad and really miss my mom when she was away, it was basically normal for me. My father was in the military too but got out when my sisters and I were younger. He was also a maintenance supervisor at the time. He took care of us during the times my mom was away. My parents always worked hard. No matter what my sisters and I did, we weren't allowed to half ass it. We had to be the best at whatever we did. There's a joke I remember from when I was younger. I think I was about thirteen. My mom asked me what I wanted to be when I grew up and I told her I wanted to be a stripper. At the time I snuck and watched The Players Club and I was fascinated by the fast money that was made by basically dancing.

Her words were, "Well you'd better be the best damn stripper out there or don't even do it."

Fast forward to the present day, I finally decided to quit my job as a Wealth Management Loan Coordinator and pursue my dream of owning my own luxe bartending company. The stress that's associated with working for somebody else's company was no longer worth it to me. Back in 2012, I was struggling to find my purpose. I felt like nothing was fulfilling to me. I just wasn't happy. I knew I should've been doing something else with my life but I couldn't put my finger on what it was. I was working this boring corporate job that I hated. I mostly hated it because I felt like I couldn't fit in. I didn't belong in that environment and everyone around me knew it. Oftentimes I was depressed because I felt like I had no purpose honestly. I knew that clocking in and out of someone's job wasn't going to complete me nor make me happy.

I decided to take a bartending class in late 2012 because for some reason, since I was a child I've always wanted to work in a club. I was really attracted to the nightlife. My first dose of the night life was when I snuck into a foam party in Seattle, Washington with some friends. You had to be eighteen to dip and twenty-one to sip. I would have never tried to drink but the freedom I felt from being in the club and being able to dance my little heart out was so attractive to me. I had so much fun that night. I'll never forget it for the rest of my days.

One of the fears I had when deciding to quit was losing the lifestyle I created based on the corporate job that paid me just enough to keep coming back. I have two loving little girls and my significant other that were all depending on me to pull my weight. It's very difficult to think about what not having the finances looks like on the other side or on the other end. I have tons of credit card debt, cars and the majority of my debt is student loans. I was pursuing a degree in finance to propel my career in corporate. Did I love it? No. But I was really good at it. Accounting came easy to me.

The closer to the time leading up to when I quit, it was inevitable that I couldn't stay any longer. The universe was definitely pushing me in that direction. It was a very difficult choice when the thought first crossed my mind. But I'll say that closer to the time when I did make the decision, I didn't even care about that anymore. I just wanted out. The amount of stress and anxiety I was feeling outweighed everything, and I needed to get it off me. Many people don't know I often struggle with bouts of depression, and it's easy for me to get in a slump and not want to do anything. I was diagnosed by my doctor back in 2008, and have been struggling with it since. Fortunately, I've been able to push through without medication or limited therapy but it hasn't been easy. My therapy is creating and now I've found something to create I release through the creation of spirited cocktails.

I really should consider more therapy but I feel bartending is a form of my therapy. I try not to wear depression on my shoulder, but my work situation was a huge contributor to my depression. I knew I wanted to be more creative and I needed to be free to do my own thing, to do what I love, not to help somebody else's dream come true. That wasn't my idea of happiness. Yes. The money was great that I was getting paid from my job and it made me feel like I had options, but having options and having control of your time are two different things. They are two different feelings.

I needed my time.

Once I decided the money wasn't going to be a huge thing, I talked it over with my significant other. As scared as I was about the potential reaction or even how to approach the conversation, I knew I had to express the way I was feeling so he could help me. Growing up, my parents communicated with one another. They were actually friends. I took that same approach within my relationship. I knew my significant other wasn't going to let me fall but I was going to be held accountable. I had to put myself in his shoes.

Would I want him to quit his career without letting me know? I would be sick at the fact we had a financial strain put on us without a plan. I would never want to put us in that situation. His support meant that he'd thought it through to the end and had a "Plan B" if all else failed. I felt comfort in knowing that I had his blessing and support; it made the transition easier. This was an important piece for me and I will say that it's important to have the support of your significant other. It was having someone in my corner that really fueled my decision to actually go through with it and quit. It felt good knowing I had support and I wasn't going to have anybody saying, "Why did you quit your job? What are we going to do now?" Instead I had somebody saying, "Hey, I got you", and, "I believe in you. I know you can do this."

With my partner being self-employed, he understood that my feelings of stress were just growing pains. Now more than ever mental health was just as important as physical health. I needed to be free. He understood what he had to do to gain success in his field. In order to enter self- employment you have to take that leap of faith, and it's never going to be a perfect time. If you feel that strongly about quitting, then quit. He made me feel much better about my decision. The time leading up to when I sent my resignation letter was kind of crazy because work was hectic at that time. I actually quit on a Monday, but the Friday before I quit, I knew that was my last day. I wasn't sure how I was going to quit or what I was going to say. But I knew at that time it was my last day. I don't know the intentions of other people. It was important to me that I didn't allow anyone to distort my decision so that's why I didn't put a two week notice in with my employer. I felt bad leaving certain individuals behind but at the end of the day it was a choice that I had to make for my well- being. It's not wise for me to make emotional decisions because I later end up regretting it one hundred percent of the time. I often move in silence for this reason. I worked like I would have on any other normal day. I got through my workload. I was able to work minimal overtime that day because I knew I wasn't coming back. I did the best I could and left my workload where somebody could easily pick it up and figure out what needed to be done. I remember calling my best friend that day and hearing her say, "Oh my gosh, you're really going to do it. You're really going to quit. Let me know how it goes."

And all day she kept asking me if I had sent the letter but I hadn't even written it yet. That next day, which was a Saturday, I started writing my letter of resignation. I wasn't sure how to say it without putting too much emotion in it or sounding like a cry baby. I really went back and forth with that letter. No matter how long it took me, my mind was already made up and I had checked out emotionally and physically on that Friday. This would be the first time I'd ever quit a job. I'd been laid off one time, but this was the first time I had "The Dream Job."

A lot of people would probably question my sanity for quitting. I had a 401k that was the bomb, good benefits and the pay was on point. I didn't share my decision because I knew in my heart that many people wouldn't really understand anyway.

Mr. Barrtenderr was my baby. I nurtured it so it could grow into what it is today. I took care of it like it was my own child. Always giving it attention and missing it when I wasn't around it. I knew the efforts, research and knowledge I dedicated to my company. I knew my skills and capabilities that I brought to the table were top tier compared to my peers. I believed in my company, Mr. Barrtenderr, so much I was ready and willing to risk it all. I couldn't waste anymore of my brain cells on somebody else's dream. So I checked out. I wrote the resignation letter and I had my mother look over it because she is a word person. She helps me out a lot because I'm very passionate at times and I would have put all of that emotion on paper. My mother is my biggest fan. I know that at the beginning she may not have understood where this was going but she definitely gets it now. We are very close. Her opinion matters to me and I still need her guidance as an adult.

It's important for me to have the right support in place because there's a time and a place for everything. My resignation letter was definitely not the time to spill my heart out. She added some things and gave me her advice on things I should remove or change. By Sunday night I finally had it all together. I read over it and I read it to my significant other one last time then I hit send. When I hit send, it was official. I was finally able to move on to the next chapter of my life. Instantly I felt that a weight was lifted off of me. Although I knew it was going to cause a whirlwind in the morning, I didn't care. This was for me. I knew I wasn't going to go back. That was the end. On that Monday my supervisor called me and I told her I had no desire to be talked out of my decision. After that conversation I had to sit there and just marvel at what I had just done. I'd sealed that chapter of my life and at the same time started a new chapter and I could feel it. It was one of the most freeing things I could have done for myself. Having control of your time and being free is a blessing. It's the ultimate key of life. I was finally going to dig into my life's purpose.

Let me be real with you for a moment, this new chapter was and (sometimes still is) scary! I have to rely a hundred percent on myself, which is very scary because I know how I love naps, especially naps in the daytime. I love having the opportunity to be able to come and go as I please.

This new space in life meant I really had to manage myself and stay focused. I knew I was more than ready. I just had way more time to devote to my company now. In the business of self-employment you have to be a self starter. You have to be self motivated and find creative and productive ways to actually make money. Depriving myself of the things I want to do is the most challenging thing for me. Of course, it would be easy for me to sleep all day or hang out with friends all day but in reality that's not possible for me. I can't make money like that. I had to work because guess what; if I didn't do it, who else is going to do it? This is my company.

Before now, in the beginning of all of this, I was really studying a lot and trying to hone in on my craft. I was attempting to perfect my jello shots and learning what spirits to use to fuse flavors together. I would let my friends and neighbors try some of my jello shots and cocktails and give me feedback or criticism about them. I was focusing on this after work and on the weekends at the time, but I always found myself running out of time.

From that, I got my first opportunity to really show what I could do. The first job I ever booked was a wedding reception. At the time one of my friends presented this opportunity to me. I was certain I wasn't going to say no and once I said, yes, it was up to me to figure it out. Most people book smaller jobs, like house parties or something like that. Not me! I booked a wedding reception for one hundred and fifty people. I had no idea what I was doing. I had never done a party or anything before. I'd be lying if I said I wasn't scared to do it. I didn't want to be embarrassed and I didn't want to embarrass my friend on her big day. I know my business was depending on me to get this right. To come in contact with that many people at one time was a lot of exposure and it was just the exposure I needed to be honest. This was way bigger than the word of mouth and the Facebook photos I was using to try to get noticed.

In order to complete this task, I had to envision what I would want if I had a wedding reception of my own. I asked myself what I could do to make this wedding reception bar look fantastic and have everything that it needs. What can I do? What would I want my bar to do? How can I make this economically efficient? How can I make a little go a long way? I figured out what I was going to do and did it. One example is I made a punch instead of serving only liquor and wine. I thought about the people who like to try new things, and I also thought about the people who are unsure of what they want. Those people are willing to explore a little more. This gave the bar more options as well. The punch was a hit! To this day I have those pictures on my social media of this beautiful bar that I created. I still think about it because it was a testament to what I could do when I had almost no resources or experience. Yes, my friend did pay me but at the time I didn't know what to charge. I took a small loss for a bigger outcome.

What separates me from others is my work ethic. This was a major boost in my confidence. Not only was the bride and groom happy, their friends and family were too. I felt like I nailed it. I was on top of the world! I think, during that event

I gave out about thirty business cards to people who asked me for them and it was only up from there.

When you're first starting a new journey it requires that you take risks and just say yes then figure out the details later. I know it's scary, but you have to challenge yourself and great things come from those challenges. Diamonds are made from pressure. So think of it like, 'I don't know how to do it, but I'm going to do the best I can. And I'm going to learn from this experience and I'm going to apply it to my next opportunity.' When you do that, you'll know that either way you win.

So since then, I've been able to grow. I've been able to grow my support system and grow my customer base and grow with the people that I have professional relationships with. I couldn't do this alone. I started it alone, but now I'm not. Believe me, that makes a hell of a difference too.

Working at the local sports bar allowed me to not only make connections with people everyday but I got to practice making cocktails. Some were good, some may have been awful but I had that space to create. I started to get regular people that preferred for me to make their drinks at the bar. To me, that's how you know you got something. I had a regular tell me when I was just starting at the bar, "Don't be afraid to pour the liquor, just pour!"

I actually took that advice and I believe that was the first time I really noticed that people were watching me make their cocktails. When I bartend at bars and clubs I feel like it's the equivalent of a performance. I feel like there's Beyonce and then there's Sasha fierce or in this case Destiny and Dynasty. Sasha/ Dynasty is the equivalent of who shows up in the fast-paced high energy places and shows out. I feel like I'm not myself and I'm focused on making this time the most lucrative experience that I can. Having a safe place to figure things out and run ideas by people, make up a support system. This is important because those are the tools I use to get me to where I'm at today. Without that, none of this would be possible. It would have taken me twice as long to achieve the things I've done.

You remember when I said I couldn't have done this alone? Well, I have individuals in my circle who ride or die. Having people that may not even understand what you're doing, may not even know anything about your industry but know what looks good is very helpful too. But I had to find what I needed and be patient because this was what brought me through a lot of adverse times. I was doing research and wanted to press the gas but the timing wasn't right. Patience came from research. I kept reading that success doesn't happen overnight. That was a true sign for me.

I saw it so often that I had no other choice but to take heed to the message. Fear keeps us all from doing certain things, but I've learned to just laugh in the face of danger. I laugh in the face of danger because I know once I get through, on the other side, I'm getting my bragging rights. You just have to find your tribe, find your support system and don't quit.

I have a little saying that I always say to myself and to others who'll listen, if you don't work, it won't work. Therefore, if I don't work, it won't work. That's what keeps me going. It used to be that my favorite thing to say was, "I'm tired." I've since gotten rid of saying that statement.

I know when my body is speaking to me and when my mind is speaking to me and it's saying I'm tired. Sometimes I'm tired, it's in the middle of doing something that I need to do. So guess what? I don't just say I'm tired then get up and leave my workstation and go lay down. I push through the wall of tiredness. With anyone that has this problem you have to keep going. You can't stop in the middle of an important task. You must stay focused on the outcome because that's a part of staying prepared. Being able to recognize opportunities is also important, but you have to be ready for them when they present themselves. In my case, I have a wish list and if it falls within the realm of what I wished for, I consider it an opportunity. If I want to work with liquor brands as part of my wish list and a brand reaches out I'm going to respond and say yes no matter what the request is. This means I'm that much closer to my wish on my wish list. With all this I do get tired, exhausted, frustrated but still I push through.

Your work ethic is what's going to speak to other people and bring them to you. That is what's going to have people gravitate towards you. I always use the phrase, "Eat the Frog." I learned this in elementary school and it stuck with me. You first have to identify your frog or the most important task, and eat it first. For me, it's normally the thing that takes the most amount of time to complete. I just work on it first to try to get it out of the way. Find something to get you through because if you don't work, it won't work.

Many people may be curious about the story behind me and my company's name, Mr. Barrtenderr. I say my name because that's what people recognize me as, but it's really much bigger than me at this point. When I learned the difference between branding and marketing it all made sense. Marketing is the angel that I was using to get people to buy my service. I was already bartending at the bar and doing parties and events (not many at the beginning) but I was just using my real name as an LLC. I'm really bad at creating names and phrases for myself but this was the first time something stuck for me. Mr. Barrtenderr derived, because I wanted to find a name that encompassed what I did, but I also wanted it to be something cool and catchy and memorable.

I'm obviously a woman, but Mr. throws people off. I wanted it to be like that because I wanted people to focus on the craft and the company itself. Basically, everything else but the face behind the brand. Nobody expects it to be a black woman, nobody expects it at all. When people tag me in things on the internet they ask, "Who's the dude that's going to be bartending here? Or what's that dude's name?", or somebody will tag me and say, "Mr. Barrtenderr can bartend at your party."

The response is, "Oh, what's his number?"

I just laugh because I think it's so funny when they have no idea.

The glass ceiling I had is now broken, now the sky's my limit. I feel I've raised the bar for not only me, but for everybody in my industry. I'm contributing to changing the industry standard with my company. I know if people book with me and my company it's going to be top tier. I've since created relationships with different spirit owners. I showcase different spirit owners and the spirits by creating craft cocktails at my Mixology classes that I hold. I am a certified bartending teacher and I teach bar education. I certify my own bartenders and I show them the way. I don't do this alone. Every day that my team and I go outside and we take down a huge job, our guests and our employers are pleased. That's how my team and I win.

I am ten toes down for myself and for my company, Mr. Barrtenderr. I had to learn that you can overcome anything if you get out of your own way.

Being on that job didn't give me the satisfaction, drive, nor the time I needed for myself to thrive. I'm now able to recognize when I have to make certain decisions. Stop thinking and just do it. If not you will think yourself right back into the same position that you were in. Dig in and create your path. You must do some soul searching if you don't know what your path is, but once you find your path, you work at it, you break that glass ceiling and you set the bar for your new life of success.

"Stop thinking and just do it. If not you will think yourself right back into the same position that you were in. Dig in and create your path. "

DESTINY WHITEHEAD

3

DETERMINED TO BE MORE
THE PATH TO BECOMING UNSTOPPABLE

"If there is no struggle, there is no progress."
—Frederick Douglass

SHEVONICA M. HOWELL, ED.S., M.B.A

DEDICATION

My chapter is dedicated to those that don't just talk a good game but play in the game. My chapter is also dedicated to those that cringe when they hear, "It's not about what you know, but who you know."

The term, Ten Toes Down, for me represents who I am on a daily basis. I am the family member that loves unconditionally, the friend whose motives aren't questioned, and the team player that goes all out for the team. I pray that my chapter motivates you to stay the course, inspire you to keep pushing, and encourage you to

ALWAYS bet on YOU!

My life from seven to eighteen was a roller coaster ride, to say the least. I was learning to love who "I thought" loved me. I was learning to deal with adversity, rejection, and life challenges, from dealing with Daddy issues, to being too naive to know everyone that told me that they cared wasn't always legit.

I was blessed to have a family that genuinely loved me unconditionally and did what they could to make life as manageable as possible.

Now, as a mother, Army veteran, motivational speaker, Literacy Coach, Chief Executive Officer, school founder and grandmother of two, I often reminisce about how my life has come full circle. Let me introduce myself, starting from elementary school and moving right up until my first year of college. I was Shevonica from Sherwood Forest and Caravan Trail, but everyone has always called me Tiny. My Mom told me I used to give away all the Little Debbie snacks to the kids in the community if they would play school with me on Saturdays and Sundays. I would be the teacher and they would be my students. She never told me I taught a certain subject, but I'm sure reading and mathematics were the favorite subjects I was teaching back then. I can clearly recall my upbringing as a child born in the seventies.

I was in the house before the streetlights were on, riding my bike with friends as a past-time and loving cartoons and all the shows on TV that gave life lessons to keep you on the straight and narrow. Honestly, the shows that shaped my life were *Good Times*, the *Cosby Show*, *227*, the *Facts of Life* and many others. I could relate to each of those shows because the experiences of the characters hit home in many ways. For instance, although it seemed as if the Evans family continued to struggle financially and dealt with issues of being "Black in America," they continued to love their family through it all. Just that alone uplifted my spirits. Now the Cosby Show allowed me to dream of being a successful parent once parenting became my reality. As far as 227 and the Facts of Life were concerned, I remember wanting to be just as feisty as Tootie and just as popular and respectable as Brenda growing up.

I also had instructors that played an integral part whom I looked up to. It makes me smile when I think about the day one of my favorite teachers reached out to me in 2017. She informed me via Facebook messenger that she was a fan of my work in the community with our youth. For me, that moment was extremely defining to say the least. I was fairly popular in middle and high school, but it had nothing to do with being a participant in after school parties or ball games. It was more to do with being friendly, helpful, and concerned about earning no less than a "C" in all courses.

I have always loved people, I have been an optimist, I have never been one to drink or smoke, and all officers have always been officer friendly. At forty seven, everything is exactly the same except the latter.

It was Easter Sunday in 1992 and at eighteen my thought process drastically changed. Even after Rodney King was beaten to a pulp, no one could tell me anything wrong about Officer Friendly. I just couldn't wrap my mind around the fact of officers doing anything wrong! I thoroughly believed that officers were only serving and protecting EVERYONE! I didn't believe any officer could be racist or prejudiced. I just thought they were treating all folk the way they would want to be treated. No one could tell me there was not a valid reason for the many beatings of blacks or other unfair incidents at the hands of those that were hired to serve and protect us all.

I held on to that belief until I was forcefully removed from the second story apartment building my family and I lived in. That officer and the other eight to nine officers disrespected me and my family that day. It wasn't warranted, expected, appreciated, or lawful. The officers ran into our apartment without a warrant! My family was sound asleep when the officers barged inside. They illegally ran into our home with guns drawn and wreaked havoc. They were real life bullies, gang members that could care less about my love for them or the reason for them disrupting our household that day was for a minor infraction. My hands and feet were attached with zip ties. I was thrown next to the squad car until I was thrown into the back seat, heading to jail or so I thought.

No, that would have been too easy! I didn't make it to the jail house until after I was taken to the back of the movie theater that was located at the corner of Atlantic Boulevard and Southside Boulevard! Oh yeah, Officer Friendly (Jacksonville's current Fraternal Order of Police President) decided to wait for his sergeant to get there to get his report as perfect as possible.

Twenty years of my life from that day was hell. I became the walking target for depressive moods and anxiety that I couldn't shake. I would cry, scream, and fight off tears of hurt, anger and the hate of myself. How could I be so stupid? How in the hell did I not see that Officer Friendly was a set up from the beginning? How did I think Rodney King could have done anything so wrong to be beaten so severely? What was I thinking?

As it was all happening on that horrible day, I remember thinking this was going to affect my mental health for the rest of my life, and it did. To be arrested and humiliated by cops that illegally forced their way into our home while chasing someone they released on his own recognizance was a nightmare. I was clearly in the wrong place at the wrong time!

By the way, after posting bail later that night, I went back to Bethune Cookman to finish my first year of college! Unfortunately, I never went back to Bethune Cookman after returning home from summer break that same year. Instead, I became an unwed mother wanting to prove that dropping out of college after my first year to focus on being a dedicated full-time Mom would be possible and rewarding. I remember wanting to show the world that deciding to have my baby wouldn't only be a delightful challenge, but also a blessing.

Now, don't get me wrong! I knew my decision wouldn't be an easy feat and, in all honesty; my initial plans failed . DRASTICALLY! I went from enrolling back in college (Jones College) in the fall of 1992 to dropping out again after the first semester. I was overwhelmed with fear and exhaustion, but still hopeful to someday hear my child say, "Mom, I am forever grateful for my up-bringing. You taught me right from wrong. You let me know that all choices require consequences and most importantly, I am proud of you and glad that you are my mom!"

I remember my decision to become the mother and father to a baby boy that was born in March of 1993. I was scared out of my wits and once my dad and stepmom pulled up to the front entrance of Memorial Medical Center on University Boulevard to take me and my child home for the night, I vividly remember asking myself, "Where in the hell is he going and what have I done?" Not knowing how to be a parent. Not having my own place to stay, car to drive, job, the experience of being anything more than a babysitter from time to time; I was lost, confused and truly in fear of knowing that this was a "consequence" that would take me years to master. I had no clue of what to do! I just wanted to close my eyes and wake up from what many would bet would be my forever failure.

But you know what? As time went on, that baby boy grew and I became wiser, smarter and more confident in being the mother I wanted and needed to be. I had no doubt I would survive! I was determined to excel, and nothing would stop me! In the fall of 1993, my son was five months old and I was determined to push forward. So, I re-enrolled back in school with the notion of being the best I could be as a mother and full-time college student. I applied at Jones College for an associate degree in Marketing and that was only because the program seemed manageable.

I remember the catalogue for the college was written in a way of allowing me to figure out just how much time it would take to receive the degree and it also gave a description of just how many courses I could take to complete the program in less time if I enrolled as a full-time student. The majority of the other students in my classes were in their thirties or forties and focused on earning their Bachelor's degree, but I didn't want to bite off more than I could chew.

I figured that if I decided to go on for my Bachelor's degree in the future; I could eventually. But completing the Associate degree was a minor accomplishment I wanted to complete first. Well, I did just that!

I was in school Monday through Friday (full-time), my

mom, Aunt, and one of my favorite cousins were my son's official babysitters, and I used my financial aid stipends to save up enough money to purchase a vehicle to get me back and forth from point A and B. Prior to purchasing a vehicle, I remember being proud about walking from Caravan Trail off Atlantic Boulevard all the way to Jones College. Jones College had two campuses, but I attended the campus that was located at the bottom of the Mathews Bridge off Arlington Expressway. I earned all A's and B's while attending Jones College for the second time around. I earned my Associate degree in Marketing, and I was confident enough to jump right into the Bachelor of Science degree that I earned a year later with honors!

Feeling confident as a single mom and new college graduate, I applied for a plethora of jobs from school teacher to H.R. manager to restaurant staff. I got my foot in the door with a nursing home and the experience allowed me to know that although I have always been a lover of people, that the healthcare field wasn't for me. Ironically, during that stint in the nursing industry I learned more than just being of assistance to those in need. Unfortunately, I learned it's not about what you know but who you know.

I initially started at the nursing home as a unit clerk, I received a promotion a few months later, and was surprisingly demoted in less than a year. But truthfully, that situation taught me to be prepared and ready for the unexpected. I was no longer the lost, unwed nineteen-year-old mother with no clue of my next steps in life; but I believed in myself enough to know I couldn't be stopped! I was a new college graduate that chose the Unit Clerk position as my first job right out of graduating from college.

For one, I felt the title alone was snazzy, and I was also satisfied with my salary. The fact that being promoted within the nursing industry was on my to do list as well, working full time hours was too easy. I was able to meet and assist families of loved ones that were hospitalized in the nursing home, and I continued to learn different aspects of the nursing field from my colleagues. To my surprise, I would hear words that made me feel even more confident as a proud, single mother that had the responsibility of living a life that my child and future child(ren) would be proud of.

Approximately eight months to a year as the unit clerk, I was informed that another position had become available that would be filled internally, and that my colleagues were mentioning me as being the best candidate for it. There was such a humbling feeling that came over me!

To be honest, I was afraid of accepting the position, but anxious to at least try at it. The open position was for a human resources clerk and although I had no experience in the position, I was willing to learn. Another thing, being in the human resources position allowed me to rub elbows with upper management because it was a position of responsibility over the company's employee records. Guess what? My position required annual performance evaluations that rated the work completed in the position. Not only would my department be evaluated, but each of the management positions within the departments would also receive an evaluation. The ratings given for the performance evaluations were an average rating, a superior rating, or a below average rating. I accepted the position, worked ten to fourteen hours a day for three to four months, and received a rating that blew the minds of everyone involved. including me! I received a superior rating, but I also received a demotion not even a week later.

All along there was another candidate chosen for the human resources department, but her title would be Human Resources Manager not clerk. I received a rude awakening! I was merely offered the HR clerk position for purposes of cleaning up the mess the former Human Resources Manager made before I was given the task. Welp! As I often say, two tears in a bucket and that is merely to keep my sanity! Any who, keep in mind I had also applied for other positions around the city with numerous companies before I accepted the unit clerk position.

Therefore, I was truly elated to receive a call back from the school board about becoming a teacher at that time and truthfully, I was sold! I was informed I was chosen to participate in a panel interview that would consist of a Principal, an Assistant Principal, two other administrators and me, of course. During the interview, I was questioned about my techniques for handling discipline. They inquired about my reasoning behind wanting the position to teach, and one statement/compliment in general was something on the line of me being informed that I had a certain "aura" about myself that would be refreshing to have as an instructor.

I smiled from ear to ear, thinking my true calling as instructor was obviously shining through at that time. But you know what? Even before that statement was given, I just knew I was going to get the job and I did! Mind you, I had enough college credits (degree) to accept a full-time teaching position a year prior, but I accepted a full-time substitute position to teach instead. My thought process was to be a substitute first and learn what teaching was about from those that were already in the field. I would then take what I liked from experienced instructors and tweak and/or delete what I didn't like. Listen, all businesses have a copycat! But your thought process should always be that your copycat is unique because it is yours and stick to it!

For me, each book I have published is a best seller because it's mine. My school is award winning because my passion is in it and I have proof of the lives I have changed. Bottom line, you must be loud, bold, and sure of why you do what you do. Not only that but having strategies and a game plan in place to ensure success is key. And more importantly, some professions should never be about the monies received but the lives being shaped, changed, and saved.

Now, fast forward a bit. I genuinely enjoyed my first year as a full-time instructor and I was elated to find I had been chosen as one of the Teacher of the Year semi-finalist. I didn't earn the title when the tallies were counted but to learn that the other instructors that made the Finals had been teaching approximately fifty-five years between them was my prize! Oh … how excitingly honored and humbled was I to learn of this news? Little old me, the unwed, first year college drop-out that was almost lost . was in the running to be the Teacher of the Year against dedicated, experienced instructors. I taught as a full-time substitute from 1996 to 1997. From 1997 – 2000, I taught as a full-time sixth grade math instructor under a temporary certificate. I never passed the Professional Educator's Exam before my temporary certificate ended, so I did the next best thing to survive . As a twenty-seven-year-old single mom, I joined the military.

After meeting with a recruiter that was a friend of my family, I decided the $10,000 sign-on bonus, rank of E4 (Army Specialist), and an all-expense paid vacation [if you will] would be the out I needed. Prior to joining the military, I started falling back into a deep depression. I was feeling like my son was stuck with a failure for a mom. I couldn't control my anxiety, the crying spells, or the hurt sitting in the bottom of my belly. I wanted to die. I wanted to be free from the hurt and disappointment I felt. I wanted to once again prove that I could be something and once I thought of all the perks that came along with becoming a soldier was icing on the cake.

He told the truth! My recruiter told the truth! And although I knew that my contract for enlisting into the military was true, having the money deposited into my bank account as soon as I completed basic training in Fort Jackson, South Carolina was motivation.

I had the pleasure of seeing my son, my mom, aunt and friends during the basic training ceremony and from there I went on to Advanced Individual Training (AIT) in Fort Eustis, Virginia. Basic training and AIT went by quickly, but I cannot lie, getting on the plane headed to my duty station in Kaiserslautern, Germany had me hoping for a miracle of some sort. I just wanted to be great. Yeah, like G.I. Jane but as G.I. Shevonica! It's hard to explain but I actually did well as a new soldier. I learned a lot from my peers, and I had the pleasure of working in areas as a soldier that was sure to give me the skills, experiences, and know-how to be an effective leader in the long run.

Unfortunately, I knew within the first year of joining that military life wasn't for me. I did complete one enlistment in the United States Army, but I was honorably discharged in August of 2003, after two years, six months and fifteen days of superior service. The long work hours, mandatory days away from my family, and the uncomfortable weather conditions weren't for me. I still don't understand how Germany's weather is tolerable to anyone born and raised in states that are sunny year-round.

I was also blessed to earn three medals and nine coins. One of the coins I received was truly special to me because I received it from the Army Chief of Staff, General Eric Ken Shinseki. Not only was he the United States Army Chief of Staff, but knowing he was also the first Asian American to receive the rank of four-star general made me want to be more. I felt that if he could break down barriers, so could I, and I would! Shoot! To even receive a second glance for my dedication to mission accomplishment from General Shinseki changed my thought process for the better.

On many occasions I have always said to myself, "*If he or she could do it* (i.e., be successful, change lives, be a positive household name) *so could I.*"

After being medically discharged from the military, I was a bit concerned about how long it would take me to land on my feet as a civilian again. Truth be told, being financially stable was the main reason joining the military was an option. I immediately applied for jobs I felt confident in mastering. There was the bank teller position I applied for as well as two to three positions as a leasing consultant in a variety of apartment complexes in town. I received job offers for most of the positions I applied for, but I took the job for the first thing: smoking. I wanted to get back out there in the job arena and show what I had to offer!

I was the new leasing consultant of Sundance Pointe Apartments that was located at the end of University Boulevard North. I loved my job! Not only was I delighted to be of assistance to those in need of being approved for an apartment, but I felt good about the position I was in.

My leasing job lasted until 2005, when I received the call back from my dream job . Math Teacher! Once again, I was blessed with the three-year temporary teaching certificate, and I knew that passing the Professional Teachers Exam this time around would be the outcome.

REJUVENATE

In August 2005, I was hired as a sixth-grade Math instructor at Matthew W. Gilbert Middle School on Franklin Street across from Richard L. Brown Elementary School. Nobody could tell me teaching wasn't the job God gave me! I loved my job so much that I had six and treasured each as much as the others. I was a Math instructor at Gilbert, I worked as the educational liaison with Huxtable Education Group under the tutelage of Mr. & Mrs. Jason Mount, I was one of the instructors for Camp Superstar, I worked for Team Up as a tutor, I tutored students that were struggling in other classes during the year, and I was also responsible for the summer lunch program.

My life as a teacher was everything I wanted it to be! Guess what else? I made it to the Teacher of the Year semi-finalist again too! This time two years in a row. I was nominated in 2006-2007, the year I really wanted the title because not only did I think I deserved it, but it was also the year my son attended Gilbert. I was also nominated the following year, and I won (2007-2008)! I was elated, but nervous! I was elated because my wish of becoming Teacher of the Year had finally come true, but I was nervous because I knew it was a possibility that this time could easily be a rerun of the last. You know, the last time I didn't pass the Professional Teachers Exam. I was confident it wouldn't be that way; but then again, I was unsure. I cannot lie, I started to doubt myself. I started thinking the happiness I'd experienced for the past three years was sure to come to an end. But what I did do differently. is celebrate the win even if it were to end soon.

In July of 2008, I was informed I didn't pass the exam after taking it seven more times and in turn, I was stripped of my Teacher of the Year title. I lost the job I'd loved for as long as I could remember, and I was about to have to start over once again. My heart was broken. I was flabbergasted and I didn't know if I was coming or going, but God. In August of 2008, I accepted a new teaching position but in a totally different field (private school instead of public). I was the Science and Math instructor for middle and high school students, but the difference between these students and students from my past was that they had always attended private schools. The curriculum was different, the thought processes were different, and the parents were different.

When I accepted the position, I was ready to see what the end would be! I went from Teacher of the Year to just another teacher . a new teacher at a new school. I was now earning $30K less a year, but my dedication to the job was even more important. At that time in my life, I knew that not only did I want to be a great teacher, but I also wanted to prove to myself that my life had always been written.

I decided to go back to school for my MBA with the thought of being a business owner on my mind. I started the MBA program with the University of Phoenix (UOP) that same month and I completed the program in less than two years. The exciting part about earning the degree was that my high school students were graduating the same year I did, and it was only a month later in May of 2010.

Once again, I was back in my happy place! I remained as an instructor with the private school until 2011. I got my foot in the door as a Business and Math professor with Heritage Institute a few months before my assignment with the private school ended, and there was no stopping me . or so I thought.

I eventually took a sabbatical from August 2011 until I was released from my doctor's care in December of the same year. Those four months were eye-opening to say the least and I hoped to never go back to a place of wanting to belong, denial, and self-neglect would be a thing of the past. I had time to relax my mind, my body, and my soul. I had time to look back at past failures, mistakes and even the good times associated with knowing that when things are great, those great things should always be cherished. You know, I always thought treating people the way I wanted to be treated was the key to always being up and not down. Well unfortunately that wasn't it, because there is always more to the story.

As soon as I made it back from my sabbatical in Tacoma, Washington, someone from my past reached out to me. She was one of the gurus of the Small Business Administration in Jacksonville that was located off Baymeadows Road. The conversation between her and I ended with me telling her I would reach out to the organizations that she referred me to, and I did. She knew I was an Army veteran, and she also knew my zeal for being the best at everything I put my mind into being. I contacted American Corporate Partners (ACP) for mentorship purposes, and I also contacted the Veteran Women Igniting the Spirit of Entrepreneurship (V-WISE) program and the Entrepreneurship Bootcamp for Veterans with Disabilities (EBV) program, as referred. Not knowing what to expect next, I waited for confirmation stating if I was approved to participate in all or any of those programs. Sure enough, I received approval to participate in all three programs simultaneously.

I believe V-WISE reached out first offering an all-expense paid weekend in Orlando. My travel was paid in full to include my hotel stay and meals consumed while there. I had the pleasure of meeting veteran women from all walks of life and our weekend was planned for all in attendance. We were being trained to step out on faith to be entrepreneurs. We were given resources for owning businesses. We were shown networking skills, marketing skills, and we were introduced to successful entrepreneurs that were running women owned businesses. And these women had only opened their businesses just months to a few years prior. This program was much needed.

I left Orlando headed back home with a whole new mindset and a whole new agenda set for my life. Prior to the Orlando trip, I'd just come back home from Washington and had only reached out to a few prospective employers. To my surprise, I was contacted by the Business Department Chairperson of Jones College, with a position proposal. She offered me a part-time teaching position as an Adjunct for the upcoming Fall term. I accepted the position and started the job in September 2012. You would never guess such luck would come. My new supervisor, the business chairperson, asked to have a word with me right after I completed my first day on the job. She went on to offer me her job as the Business Department Chairperson due to her resigning from that position to take over as the new Dean of the College. I was dumbfounded, in awe, and extremely grateful. I cried, I laughed, we hugged, and I couldn't wait to share the news with my family and friends. I had two jobs! Two jobs that kept my spirits up for years to come.

From September 2012 until I resigned in 2013, my business cards read: "Shevonica M Howell, Business Chair/Business Professor of Jones College." I resigned from the business chair position in September and from being a professor at the end of the 2013 term in December.

My mind was made up to finally be my own boss. I placed my business plan into a competition sponsored by V-WISE and Citibank in August 2013, I started my fourth degree at Nova Southeastern University in September 2013, and received a congratulatory email in December of 2013 stating that I made it as a Semi-Finalist in the business plan competition. I remember it like it was yesterday! I told any and every one that would listen, that I would win. Yes, I remember the competition well. I was the first one to compete in the competition out of the eighteen of us chosen. I was excited. I gave it my all, but it was a good eight hour wait after I pitched my business at 8:00AM before sealing the deal. At approximately 4:30PM, I read the congratulatory email that stated Shevonica M. Howell of Academy of Scholars, Inc., would be competing for the top prize of $25.000.

The final stage of the competition wouldn't be until the following day, but I was ready for it all. I was ready before the plane landed in Long Beach, California the day before I competed in the first stage of the competition, so it was about to go down! It went a little something like this: I started the competition by setting the bar and I ended the competition with, "I am Shevonica M. Howell, founder and CEO of Academy of Scholars, Inc., in Jacksonville, FL. I am determined to be more than what they say I will be, motivated enough to push for what I want to be, and destined to be what I was born to be. A TESTIMONY!"

I received a standing ovation, and the second-place prize of $15,000 to fund my new private school. On Wednesday, September 3, 2014, I had the pleasure of opening my private school, Academy of Scholars, Inc., and at that time I was renting an 18,000 square foot building in Arlington off of Arlington Expressway. The building was a two-story that I felt was more than perfect for my school's first year as a start-up.

It included four classrooms upstairs, four classrooms downstairs, a gymnasium, my office, the front office, a security office, two female restrooms, and two male restrooms (one on each floor). We offered all core subjects to include English, Language Arts, Reading, Spelling, Mathematics, History and Science. We also offered the following elective courses: Dance, Tae Kwon Do, Art, Music, Business Literacy, and our Foreign Language course was Hebrew/Farsi. For me, I felt I'd finally succeeded … that I'd finally reached a goal that many felt couldn't be done (well not by me anyway).

After completing more than three years of research, to include my dedication, and my commitment to becoming a private school owner to finally earn the title, was everything! I was more than elated and within my school's third year of being open, I had a teacher in every classroom! The icing on the cake was to find out I was actually paying my instructors a salary that most private school founders weren't paying their teachers or staff. I offered many courses that weren't being offered at most private or public schools and most importantly; I wasn't only the founder, but I taught the Math and Business courses at my school as well. The skies were the limit for me, and I was Happy ... truly happy with what I'd accomplished.

I can remember feeling that every day was nothing less than a perfect day. The students were being nurtured, taught, and motivated to never give up. The instructors and staff were feeling appreciated by the students, parents, and me of course. I remember being frightened because the feeling of peace was overwhelming to say the least. It was overwhelming because every day I felt that everything about Academy of Scholars, Inc. was too good to be true. It's hard to explain, but I remember being happy, yet frightened even with my continuous faith in God.

I remember doing everything in my power to stay focused, yet my nerves were taking the best of me. But I continued to pray, I continued to move forward with what I knew was right, and I also continued to focus on learning more and more daily. And although, I can truly say that my first 540 school days as a founder was well worth the sleepless nights and adversity that came with the title, it only took a good 180 days or should I say; one official school calendar year to realize what was upon me. My first three school years as founder and CEO were a success, but I was in jeopardy of not having a place to run my school for the next school year due to finances. I only had seven to ten students in the school during the first year, monies from scholarships and cash paying parents was scarce. I guess this was one thing that I didn't research well enough. For instance, students that received scholarships from Step Up for Students could be enrolled at my school for ninety days, but if their parents withdrew them on the ninety first day, that day would place me in jeopardy of having to pay back monies I received prior to the student being withdrawn. Yeah, make that make sense!

I struggled to stay afloat as a private school founder, but I continued to run it with God's grace and mercy alone. By the time the third school year started I knew I could no longer survive as a business owner by paying more in rental fees than what was being brought in as annual earnings. I ended up closing the doors of my first rental building to house my school elsewhere.

UNEXPECTED INTERRUPTIONS

The new rental property was in the heart of a neighborhood that needed a school that was dedicated to being more than just a school. It would be a place of learning and encouragement, but it would also be a safe-haven for kids that needed more than a place to learn arithmetic. Funny thing about the second rental property was that I wasn't given approval by the city to step foot in those doors, although I had already signed a lease. The new building was known for housing one of Duval County's very first Head Start programs for more than a decade and I had no doubt about it being just as perfect as my school's first building.

Well, after moving more than $25K worth of furniture from Arlington to the Northside of town I was shocked to find that the City of Jacksonville decided to deny my request for an exception. That year, my school closed its doors. Well, something like that ... Yes, the majority of my students were withdrawn from my school. Yes, I didn't have a building to house my school and yes, I was close to being worn down mentally. But what I did was become more creative. I began writing more books, I began contacting other educational facilities and media outlets, and I started participating in numerous speaking forums to promote myself! I knew my experience, skills, and passion for teaching was the key to becoming unstoppable.

In the summer of 2019, I was offered a spot on a radio talk show to speak about my zeal for being an instructor, school founder, author, and motivational speaker. Not only did I have the pleasure of taking the radio host up on that offer, but I accepted a tutoring position that would allow me to focus on students in two grade levels that I never felt confident in teaching (1st and 2nd grade). I will never forget the year of 2019, and although I have always believed that everything in this world happens for a reason, that particular year has me believing those words even more. I met a mother of two that was caring for her children as they were in hiding from her estranged husband at that time and she had been for approximately three years prior. I shared with her my reason for agreeing to be a guest on the talk show which was to promote my school that no longer had a building.

Long story short, I met with the mother once more after that interview and everything else was like a dream come true. My school was housed in the basement of her condo and her kids were my students for that upcoming school year. The school setting was large enough for six students and I continued to promote my school during the 2019-2020 school year. I had other parents that reached out, but my two enrolled students ended up being the only students I taught for that school year. Oh yeah! I cannot forget my first and second grade students. I was also tutoring in the afternoons from Monday through Friday, after my school hours ended each week.

The 2019-2020 school year ended successfully and the students of Academy of Scholars, Inc. ended up being accepted into a prestigious private school prior to the end of that school year. Moreover, my first and second graders earned straight A's during the last nine weeks of the 2019-2020 school year, being that I had the pleasure of assisting them with completing that final nine weeks due to the COVID-19 pandemic that caused many of Duval County Public School doors to close.

From the summer of 2020 to the end of August 2020, I received a plethora of phone calls from interested parents wanting their kids to attend my school for the 2020-2021 school year. Although only two students enrolled for the 2020-2021 school year, the hours of operation, school schedule and other opportunities presented to me made the school year a winner. I had the pleasure of writing more books to add to my school's curriculum (10 total) and not to mention the YOU TEACH IT Math Study Guide that was adopted by an international after school program.

I realized that my school being closed for a spell was for me to learn that God wanted me to know just how much I had learned on my path to opening an even bigger school in my future. I went from wanting a teacher in every classroom to understanding that my many degrees in business and education had allowed me to teach all subjects successfully. I went from losing the Teacher of the Year title to becoming a private school founder, although I never passed the Professional Exam for teachers. I went from losing a school building that I was renting at a fee that was unbearable to being blessed with housing my school during the 2019-2020 school year and the 2020-2021 school year for free. In reality, for years I was down on myself for feeling like I had failed. When all along I was succeeding in more ways than one.

I am blessed and highly favored, and it is nice to know that the seeds that I continue to sow aren't in vain. And once I was able to tell my story without needing tissue, it was clear that my motivational quote fit well with my new and improved goal of becoming unstoppable!

"*I am determined to be more than what they say I will be, motivated enough to push for what I want to be, and destined to be what I was born to be...A TESTIMONY!*"

SHEVONICA M. HOWELL

II

CHANGE

"Change will not come if we wait for some other person or some other time. We are the ones we've been waiting for. We are the change that we seek."

~BARACK OBAMA

4

THE RIGHT CONNECTIONS:
UNLOCKING WHO YOU ARE MEANT TO BE

"Not everything that is faced can be changed, but nothing can be changed until it is faced."
—James Baldwin

AARON DAYE

DEDICATION

This chapter is dedicated to my mother and father, Aarona and Edward Daye and to my sister Nakkia "Nikki" Daye. Thank you for always believing in me and encouraging me to be true to myself and to be the person I want to become. I hope I'm making you all proud every day because I know they are looking down on us.
Rest in Peace Mom and Dad

As a kid growing up in Durham, North Carolina or as some of us like to refer to as the "Bull City," life seemed to be at a standstill. There were so many abandoned homes and buildings especially in parts of downtown in what used to be known as Black Wall Street, we all struggled with the idea of getting out. I would always hear that history repeats itself and you see it in culture and fashion where something from every decade always comes back as a trend. To my family, the standstill was more like a generational curse or series of bad decisions that held our family back. I was always determined to be the one to break this so-called generational curse and create a legacy for our family.

Creating a legacy sounds good but no one tells you how. There wasn't a manual with instructions on bringing your family out of poverty so my philosophy in life became I will figure it out. Growing up, my mom, sister and I lived with my grandmother when my parents divorced. I became accustomed to struggle. Seeing my mom and grandmother struggle to put food on the table and keep the power and hot water on. There were plenty of days having to wash my clothes in the sink and drying them either in the microwave or the stove trying to keep watch so they wouldn't catch on fire. I just wanted better for us.

From the age of fourteen, when I got my first job as a scorekeeper for Durham Parks and Recreation to through college working three jobs at a time while in school full-time wanting to help my family where I could. I didn't have the best grades in college mainly from always working and studying for classes and history of the fraternity I was hoping to join in-between customers and my lunch breaks. When my senior year in college came, I was so unprepared for what was next. I'd just joined the Gamma Beta Chapter of Alpha Phi Alpha Fraternity, Incorporated and had struggled all semester to maintain a C+ average. I decided to stay an extra year to get back on track and refocus on helping provide for my family. That extra year, I pulled my grades up and was about to graduate with honors. I remember wondering about the many doors this Cum Laude seal was going to open for me. For most people, the day you graduate from college is supposed to be one of the greatest moments of your life. Family members come together for one day to celebrate your accomplishments. At least that's what the pictures on social media today show us.

In the spring of 2005, I became the first person in my family to graduate from college. The day of my graduation ceremony, I found out later the announcements never made it out to other family members so only my immediate family was there for support. That morning, however, as I stumbled through the processional line slightly still reeking of last night's festivities, I pondered my next moves. It finally hit me that this was it. All of my hard work paid off. Working three jobs and being enrolled in school full-time is what led up to this moment. Suddenly my whole life and the impact others had on my life thus far began running through my mind. I thought of moments where I wanted to give up but thankfully, I hadn't.

As I walked across the stage on that hot Saturday morning of Mother's Day weekend, I accepted my degree and all I could think about in that brief moment was how proud my family was going to be of me as the first college graduate in our family. How proud my mom was going to be to see me accomplish the one thing she had always dreamed of doing herself.

After the ceremony, while searching for my family through a crowd of hundreds who had gathered to see their person graduate, I was shocked but not surprised that my sister was the only person I saw waiting for me after the ceremony. Confused as to what happened, I was informed that my grandmother had suddenly become too hot while sitting in the stands of the football stadium. At the beginning of the ceremony, she had asked my mother to take her back home so that she could cool off, according to my sister. I was upset. No, I was furious! I felt that because of the rocky relationship we had for so many years living in the same household, I thought she was making this day that should be about me about her.

With so many other families there with grandparents who were supporting their grandchild, why couldn't mine be there to support me? My mother unfortunately never made it back in time to see me actually walk across the stage. My father Edward Daye was a landscaper at my college and had to work graduation morning. I'm still not actually sure if he saw me graduate. My sister Nikki however stayed and cheered on her little brother as she had always done throughout my life. I owe my passion for photography to my sister for her support and encouragement.

My sister Nikki however stayed and cheered on her little brother as she had always done throughout my life. Some of my fondest memories growing up were always feelings of being protected by my sister. We were like most brother and sister siblings, we fought each other…a lot, but when things went wrong she was always there for me. When I got my first job, Nikki took me back and forth to work. When I wasn't feeling well Nikki took care of me. When drugs became an issue during hard times within the family, Nikki did everything she could to shelter me from it. Nikki gave me my first car, a 1990 Plymouth Sundance with a blue interior to match the exterior that I lovingly called "Blues Clues." I mean most of my early memories were with my big sister.

When I was in middle school, she worked at the local Food Lion grocery store. Every week she would bring home these disposable Kodak cameras that she would never really use. She had intentions of using them but between work, school, and church she never found the time. On the other hand, I had the time and was intrigued by them because of the memories that were created with them. Moments lasting a lifetime captured in seconds at the snap of a button. My grandmother had a box of old photographs from trips she would take with her friends when my mother was young. They weren't the best photos but they were memories she had made and I wanted to make some memories of my own. Instead of letting them sit there collecting dusk, I decided to take her half-used cameras to school and started taking photos of my friends, my little crushes and just things around me. She started noticing that her cameras would randomly disappear and then reappear somewhere near where she left them, and out of film.

When she finally decided to get the film in those cameras developed, to her surprise she was clueless as to who the people in the photos were. She wasn't mad but she knew then that if she didn't bring any home then I would continue taking them for myself. She started bringing home cameras from me almost weekly. Ironically, my family did not like taking pictures so my friends and classmates became my photo subjects. Between middle school and college, I had taken four photography classes but was mostly self-taught. When my photography instructor, mentor and University photographer, the late Robert Lawson, had photoshoots scheduled during his teaching hours, he would have me take over his class. After all, I was the photo editor of the school newspaper and a yearbook photography staff member so I felt somewhat qualified.

About two months before my college graduation, my advisor and Campus Echo Newspaper editor, Bruce dePyssler, had encouraged me and a few of the other graduating newspaper editors to continue the tradition of our predecessors and apply to the New York Times Student Journalism Institute. The NYT Journalism Institute was a fairly new fellowship program under the New York Times Company umbrella and held annually on the campus of Dillard University in New Orleans, Louisiana. We had just come back from the 2005 Historically Black Colleges and Universities (HBCU) "Excellence in Journalism" contest where the Campus Echo won a record eight first place awards. I was feeling unstoppable having contributed and earned three of the eight first place awards in categories "Best Photography", "Best Individual Photo" and "Best Feature/Arts & Entertainment Page Design" so when dePyssler told us to put a portfolio together I knew I had some good content. As the deadline to apply was approaching, I anxiously put together my portfolio including my most recent awards and some of my best photo clips from my internship at the Herald Sun Newspaper from the previous summer. I made several revisions to my essay and resume and was ready to send out my application packet. I was just shy of the deadline not because I'd procrastinated this time but I'd made so many revisions to both my essay and resume trying to perfect them for whomever would be reviewing it.

About a month later, I received the news that I was one out of four photographers of the thirty students selected from Historically Black Colleges and Universities (HBCU) from across the country to be a part of the third class of the New York Times Student Journalism Institute. This was the first year that two students, my colleague Sheena Johnson and I, were selected from NCCU to attend the institute.

Two weeks after graduation, Sheena and I were off for New Orleans, Louisiana for this intense, fast-paced but all-expense paid journalism training program. We both had just received the 2005 Chancellor's Soaring Eagle Award during an Honors Convocation before graduation so we were ready to go out and represent NCCU amongst the other HBCUs at the Institute. I was excited but nervous at the same time because I never imagined that this was where journalism would take me. I recall during the second semester of my freshman year, I quit my college newspaper because I felt I wasn't going to ever work for a newspaper after graduation so why bother putting in the work. The day I quit, my advisor Bruce DePyssler gave me a look of disappointment with a slight smirk and said, "Ok, but you'll be back." Fast forward 4 years and here I was an award-winning photojournalist about to travel nearly thirteen hours away to dive head first into this journalism program. The Institute brought in some of the leading journalism professionals from the Times Company regional newspapers including such papers as The Boston Globe, The New York Times and The Times-Picayune Newspapers.

For two weeks, from sun up to sun down we lived and breathed journalism gaining the most invaluable writing, editing, newsroom and field experience covering stories drawn from the historical setting of New orleans. Two other students from my college, both photographers, Rashaun Rucker, class of 2003, and Denita Smith, class of 2004, had previously been selected for the Institute each year prior and had done very well for themselves. Rashaun had gone on to become a photojournalist for the Detroit Free Press following the Institute and with the impact he left behind, I realized I needed to work even harder than everyone else. At the end of the program, every class produced a newspaper with each photographer writing a full-page photo essay on a topic of their choosing. By the end of the program, my class had produced a 28-page newspaper. I had twenty-four images throughout the entire newspaper, far more than any of the other photographers including the front-page lead photo. This was a big deal because it would forever be seen as the lead photograph to represent the hard work of my class as a whole. I was so proud of the work that we had accomplished as a class and felt even prouder not just because I had the lead art but because I was representing my alma mater North Carolina Central University nationally now.

That summer after I got back to North Carolina, I was riding on cloud nine feeling like I left my final mark on the award-winning Campus Echo student newspaper and was proud to represent my alma mater. It was my moment to make sure people knew North Carolina Central University was here and NC A&T was not the only HBCU in the entire state of North Carolina. I stayed in touch with Christine Bence who was a Human Resources director for the New York Times Regional Media Group based in Tampa, Florida and my institute photography editor José Lopez, a photography editor for the New York Times. About three weeks had gone by and I received an email from Christine connecting me with Rob Witzel, the director of photography for The Gainesville Sun newspaper located in Gainesville, Florida. Apparently, my hard work at the NYT Institute hadn't gone unnoticed and I was informed that I had been chosen for an internship opportunity with one of their regional newspapers.

A few days later, Witzel called me about the internship. I remember standing in the kitchen of my grandmother's house when the phone rang. I let it ring at least three or four times just looking at the phone trying to decide how to answer the phone. In my mind, I was thinking I'm a little over a month out as a new college graduate and this call could determine the next phase of my life. I answered the phone saying, "Hello?" trying my best to not sound anxious even though I was. Witzel says to me, "Hey Aaron this Rob Witzel at the Gainesville Sun in Gainesville, Florida, how are you doing?" I wanted to respond really casually but the anxiety had taken over thinking about how important this call was going to be.

I replied, "Oh hey Rob. I'm doing well, and yourself?"

He replied, "Good. Listen. I received a call from some colleagues at the Times raving about how good you did at the institute. I wanted to invite you down for an internship at the Gainesville Sun." I remember him saying, "The internship is with the Sun. We are starting a new newspaper called The Gainesville Guardian Newspaper that would focus on news in the Black community of Eastside of Gainesville. You would be the main photographer and it would only be part-time so about twenty to thirty hours a week. I can't tell you right now how much you would be making because we're still working out the details of the newspaper but if you're interested we'd love to have you."

I didn't know what questions to ask, all I was thinking was I had two choices; either take the internship, work even harder than I did at the institute and see what happened, or to stay in NC, find a job working for the city and just figure it out. I'd never heard of Gainesville before but after the rigorous newsroom training of the NYT Institute in New Orleans I thought I was ready for anything.

I saw this internship as my chance to get away from home and not be trapped like my mother often felt. She would sometimes tell me how different she thought our lives would have been if my grandfather James "Aaron" Stewart was still alive. I never got a chance to meet the relative I was named after, unfortunately because he passed away when my mother was only thirteen years old. My mom felt my grandmother Lois blamed him for leaving her to raise my mom alone after he passed. Because of that, she felt my grandmother held her back from chasing her dreams of studying fashion at an out-of-state college. She started college but met my father and neither of them finished their education. They got married, worked random jobs to support us. My mother became a social worker for the Food Stamp office and always seemed unfulfilled.

Because the relationship between my grandmother and I was always confrontational, she didn't want that for my sister and I. She felt that because I reminded so much of him and that had to be the reason we didn't get along. Looking back, I think that was why she wanted my sister and I to always go after our dreams and be the best at whatever we decided.

I thought about that when I received the call about the internship. I was the first to graduate from college, the first and only in my immediate family to join a Black Greek-letter fraternity (Alpha Phi Alpha Fraternity, Inc.) and the first to be moving out of state. I had never lived away from home before even throughout my years in college, let alone had even thought about living out of state. To me and everyone I knew who had never even been that far away, we all ignorantly thought the entire state of Florida was like Miami. In my mind, it was bright lights, beaches, bikinis and alligators, and this was my chance to leave. My parents, unfortunately, never really prepared my sister and I to live on our own. After my parents divorced when we were just kids, they both returned home to live with our grandmothers. I couldn't blame them too much for not teaching us real life skills and how to be on our own. I had no choice but to figure it out along the way. I adapted that as my "unofficial motto". I wanted to go to art school after I graduated from high school but we couldn't afford the tuition so it forced me to decide if going broke to go to school was worth it because my McDonald's scholarship application was never submitted by my manager.

Four years of working at this fast food lifestyle with the goal of going to college someday, somewhere other than in Durham, and I had nothing to show for it. It motivated me to work hard and not rely on others to make a way. When I joined the Kappa Alpha Psi Beautillion to raise money for college, I thought this would be the key to my success. I was literally begging people for financial help and had barely raised enough money to afford a semester at the local community college. I was not going to allow anything to stop me. That only motivated me to figure it out. I found out that one of my dad's friends, Elton, had a girlfriend named Teresa who worked in the financial aid office at NCCU. I didn't know her and barely knew Elton at the time but she was heaven sent. Through that connection, I was allotted the opportunity to go to college. Obstacles came and went but I faced them and always figured out a way when the path was unclear.

I attempted to get my affairs in order and thankfully while I was in New Orleans I was having a transmission rebuilt and installed into the first car I ever purchased. Back in college, around my sophomore year, I spent my entire refund check to purchase my first car, a used red and black 1990 Mitsubishi Eclipse. Back then at HBCUs specifically, your refund check was everything. People would arrive on campus sometimes at four or five o'clock in the morning lining up outside the bursar's office waiting for them to open to receive their refund check. I remember watching the line of people spread throughout the hallways and the stairwell of the NCCU Administration Building and eventually wrapping around the outside of the building and forming a line through campus. It was as if it was HBCU Stimulus Day and they were giving out money and we were all waiting for our piece of the pie. Most of us had already spent our refund checks before we even received them and I had a plan for mine. That car was everything to me. It was my first ever major purchase and I felt like a Speed Racer behind the wheel of my very own sports car. It didn't matter to me that it was under my mom's insurance, I bought it so it was mine.

A year later, the transmission went out and I had to park it, I was heartbroken. After three years of sitting outside the front yard of my grandmother's house, I'd finally saved up enough money to get my transmission fixed. I'd been working three jobs (Athlete's Foot, Victoria Secrets and The Campus Echo) simultaneously while in school full-time and used most of my final refund check to have the transmission rebuilt.

Sometime after I'd returned home from the New York Times Student Journalism Institute in New Orleans, the Eclipse was ready for pickup. I was all set for the big journey to Gainesville for my internship, or so I thought. One day I was driving my car home from saying goodbye to friends. I was getting I-85 onto the Durham Freeway when the engine and oil lights lit up on my dashboard. The car I'd just spent nearly two thousand dollars on a transmission on was now spilling old oil along the Durham Freeway. Apparently, the mechanic shop never thought to check the oil even though they knew it had been sitting there for a few years. The one thing the NYT Institute taught me was you needed transportation to be ready at all times for a story to break and it was a harsh reality making that phone call to Witzel to explain my car situation and not being able to get there on time for my internship. He thankfully told me that Brian Kratzer, the new director of photography, was starting in August. He said to stay in touch and keep him posted on my car situation but to get there when I could.

For the next few weeks, I was jobless but did everything I could think of to raise money for a new car to get to this internship in Florida. With my birthday coming up that June, I made so many calls to family and friends and to anyone I met along the way that told me I would be someone one day. I elicited help from anyone who'd listen so that I could get this car running. I was determined to get to Florida. Everywhere I went I carried this five gallon water jug asking for donations as I repeatedly shared the story of my car oil on the freeway and needing to get to my internship.

One day while walking home from campus, down Fayetteville Street, I decided to ask random people for change. I ran into a buddy of mine Dexter Scott the owner of Earthquake Productions near his office on Fayetteville Street. I met Dexter when I was in high school at the beginning of my party promotion days, while I was working under local event promoter and radio personality Brian Dawson. Dexter would provide the DJs and sound for all my events and for the "10:40 Class Break" on campus of my alma mater, North Carolina Central University (NCCU) every Tuesday and Thursday. That would be our time to catch up. Dexter knew about my photography at NCCU because he hosted the annual CIAA Step Show I would shoot.

That particular day, Dexter invited me to his office to share my story. I told him how I'd put everything I had into this car and after I got my internship the car failed me so not to give up on this opportunity, I was doing what I had to do to raise the money to get to Florida for my internship. Dexter pulled out his checkbook and like a human angel he wrote me a check for five hundred dollars and told me, "Take this and go and live your dreams," and that was exactly what I intended to do. It took everything in me not to tear up in front of him but no one has ever shown this much kindness towards me. He believed in me and I was determined not to let him or my family down.

By mid-July, I had raised about a thousand dollars and was finally ready to get a used car. The college chapter advisor of the Gamma Beta Chapter of Alpha Phi Alpha Fraternity, Incorporated and the former NCCU Chief of Police McDonald Vick reached out to a family friend who owned a small used car dealership in Eutawville, South Carolina. Chief Vick told me he had explained my situation and gave me his contact information and said I just needed to get there. I connected with him, used the dollars I raised to buy a money order and convinced my frat brother and friend Maurice Atkinson, II to drive me almost four hours to this used car dealership in small town Eutawville, SC where the population according to the 2019 U.S. Census was 290 people. We got into the car and hit the road for Eutawville. We went straight to the car dealership somewhere near Old Number Six Highway in South Carolina.

When we arrived at the car dealership, I immediately had my eyes on a gold 2001 Honda Accord. I figured since I was an Alpha that the car was perfect for me. The car dealer quickly told me that Chief Vick told him my situation but the Honda was definitely out of my price range. After taking time to look at the slim pickings of cars he had on the lot, he told me there was a green sedan I could pay for in full. The sedan he was referring to was a green 1997 Dodge Neon Highline Sedan with mint green cloth interior. With limited options and eager to get to my internship, I signed the paperwork and paid for the vehicle and began to follow my fraternity brother to the interstate to head back to North Carolina. I looked at Maurice and said let's roll baby! I got in the car, put the keys in the ignition. I quickly realized this didn't have a functioning car horn, radio or air conditioning but it did however come with a remote starter which I thought was just a keyring. I immediately got out of the car and went back to the car dealer to tell him about its flaws and that I was going to Florida and at the very least I needed air conditioning. He politely told me that all sales were final so I had no choice but to take the car I had purchased and to get ready for Florida.

As soon as we got onto I-95 North, all four of the car hubcaps flew off the tires in every direction. I was still stuck on not getting the Honda Accord that I wasn't as appreciative of this blessing so when those hub caps flew off it was as if God was reminding me of what he had just blessed me with. You know how parents often discipline their children reminding them that how easily things are given that it can be even easier to have them taken away. I flashed my lights to signal Maurice and pulled over to the shoulder of the interstate. As Maurice was getting out of the car, he looked at me with a confused expression as if he really was seeing things and said to me in his thick New York accent, "Yo A, I'm not bugging but did I really see what I think I saw?"

As I looked down the interstate neither of the hubcaps were in sight. I had no explanation for him. There was no need to confirm the missing hubcaps, it was quite obvious that not one, not two but all four of the hubcaps were missing.

We got back on the road to head back to North Carolina praying nothing else went flying before I could make it. When I got home, I called Witzel immediately and told him I could start on August 1st. I was optimistic in thinking that if this was how the journey began then it could only be up from here. I soon realized this wasn't a journey but the beginning of an adventure.

The day had finally come for me to leave for my internship. I'd asked so many people to believe in me and now it was time to believe in myself. The date was Sunday, July 31st, 2005. I was late getting on the road for Gainesville trying to spend as much time with my family as possible. I had my suitcase packed and loaded with all four pages of the from Durham, North Carolina to Gainesville, Florida MapQuest directions that I had printed since GPS on cell phones were not a thing yet. I had an eight hour drive ahead of me. My mom had fixed me a to-go plate, gave me the longest hug she had ever given me and told me to be careful. She would always worry about me and I never made it easy for her not to. At the time, I didn't realize when I left this would be one of the last times I would be able to call Durham home again. Within the year, my grandmother's Dementia had become even worse than before and my mother was unable to afford to work and maintain the upkeep of the home to an adequate standard of living while taking care of my grandmother.

After spending everything I had on the Dodge Neon, my family gave me what they could to help get me to this internship. I left Durham headed for Gainesville with seventy five dollars in my pocket. I might have stopped at every rest area after every state line for a bathroom break or just to take a quick nap. This was the first time I had driven this far from home and literally by myself with not even a radio to keep me company so the quietness quickly got the best of me. I arrived in Gainesville, Florida about four o'clock in the morning but here was the thing, I never made any living arrangements. I was so caught up with trying to raise money and find a car just to make it to my internship that I never worked out where I was going to stay when I got there. I pulled up at the intersection of SW 13th Street and Waldo Road, an intersection that will take you to the next town over in any direction you decide to go.

It was so dark and so late that I made a left turn as if to go back out of town towards the Micanopy area. I pulled up to the first hotel just south of town to the Budget Inn. After stopping to fill up for gas once and food from the McDonald's dollar menu, I had about $55 dollars left in my pocket and spent all of that on one night's stay at the Budget Inn. I still can't believe they charged me for a full night at four am but I was starting my internship within a few hours and needed to get some rest.

The next day was Monday morning and with only a few hours of sleep, I was still tired from the night before. I got up, wiped the sleep from my eyes and went straight for the shower. I didn't want to be late even though the hotel was literally only a two minute drive away from the newspaper office. I rushed to get dressed, grabbed my bags because I only had enough money for one night, loaded up the Neon and slowly made the short drive to the newspaper office. As I was driving to the newspaper for my big first day, I remember reflecting on the conversation I had with my dad after accepting the intern position. I asked him if he'd ever been to Gainesville or at least heard of it?

He looked me dead in my eyes and said, "They have alligators walking in the streets in Gainesville, just be careful you don't want to get eaten." I was gullible enough to believe him and was instantly afraid. I felt like I needed to have my head on a swivel riding through town.

I pulled into the newspaper parking lot and as soon as I put the car in park immediately, I had this overwhelming feeling of nervousness come over me. The moment had finally come and all I had to do was get out of the car and walk through the front door. I said a prayer and right afterwards began saying, "Just get out of the car Aaron." I continued to repeat it back to myself over and over again until I actually got the nerves to open the door and get out of the car.

With somewhat fresh eyes still tired from the long journey just the night before, I walked through the front door with a huge smile on my face ready to start this next chapter. I greeted the receptionist saying, "Good morning my name is Aaron Daye and I'm here to start my internship in photography."

With an unexpected look, she politely told me to have a seat and that someone would be with me shortly. I looked at the empty row of seats and looked back at her and she gave me the slightest head nod like an unofficial seal of approval as I walked over to have a seat. I sat eagerly waiting to meet the person I had been speaking with over the last few months. As I looked up I noticed a young guy wearing a turquoise colored linen shirt and khakis coming down the stairs.

He walked towards me, extended his hand and said, "Hey Aaron, I'm Doug Finger, one of the photographers here at The Sun." I wish I could remember what he said after that. I was just somewhat shocked that the director or I guess now the Assistant Director of Photography I'd been speaking with was nowhere to be found. Doug was nice and all but Witzel had been my only contact at the newspaper so I was a bit disappointed that he wasn't there to meet me on my first day.

I followed Doug through the newsroom as he gave a quick L-shaped tour from the door to the photography department. When we walked into the office, I was introduced to staff photographer Michael Weimer as the new intern. I remember the surprised look on his face as he said, "I didn't know you were starting this week. Witzel's on vacation and Kratzer took his family to Disney World before starting work and hadn't made it in yet."

He pointed to a row of iMac's and told me they were the intern computers. I was confused like was this what I had fought so hard to get down to Florida for to just sit at a computer and wait? As I walked over to the computer, I tried to be optimistic thinking *well at least I had a window and the staff photographers did not.* My optimism was instantly shattered when I looked out the window and all I could see were trees and a newspaper truck. Doug noticed the look on my face and said, "We just use those windows to light the office." I instantly found myself frowning.

Before I knew it, I was spending my first days checking emails, updating my Facebook page and looking for somewhere to stay. On the bright side, I'd started my internship, well sort of, but I still hadn't worked out my living arrangements. Needless to say, my first few days in Florida weren't what I expected.

By the end of my first day, I'd mapped out apartments in the area closest to the newspaper office just in case I ran into car trouble again. Five pm came and went, then six pm, then seven pm. It was dinner time and before I knew it, it was almost ten pm at night and I was still at the newspaper office and broke. I was hungry and had no family or no friends in the area. I mean I literally had no place to go. I did the only logical thing I could think of so I slept in the Dodge Neon. It was the beginning of August and that Florida heat was on the rise so I cracked the front two windows, set the alarm on my phone and went to sleep hungry in the front seat in the parking lot of the newspaper.

The next morning, I crawled out of my car, stretched my legs, walked over to the lunch bench near the back entrance of the newspaper office and sat and waited for someone to open the door. I didn't want anyone to see me wearing the same clothes I had from the day before, not as if anyone had noticed or even knew who I was yet but I didn't have an ID badge or door key so I waited. I walked in behind one of the morning reporters and rushed into the downstairs bathroom. That particular bathroom had a shower but I didn't trust it because it was in a dark corner of the bathroom and looked too similar to a horror film and I had come too far to go out like that. I took a sink bath, got dressed, put my clothes in my backpack and went upstairs to work like it was just another day.

I spent the morning calling around to the apartment complexes I'd researched the day before. At lunchtime, I drove to Arbor Park Apartments a few blocks away from the newspaper office. It was within walking distance to the newspaper, in case something happened to the car again. I walked into the office and explained to the leasing agent my situation with The Gainesville Sun that I was here for an internship that would be a job with an extension of the newspaper called The Gainesville Guardian Newspaper. The leasing agent heard my story and gave me an amazing deal on a one year lease for a two bedroom apartment as a Gainesville Sun employee. Thankfully, they were so anxious to lease the apartment that I didn't have to pay a security deposit. That worked for me because I was broke!

I told the leasing agent to give me a moment to step out and make a phone call. I stepped outside of the leasing office to call my sister and get her advice on the apartment. As I was pacing around the parking lot, I explained my current living situation and exactly what Witzel told me before starting my internship that it would be ten weeks paid, and afterwards I would be working for The Guardian Newspaper, and I just didn't know how much money I would be making. As she told me her concerns and tried to figure out why I didn't have any money left, I noticed a guy wearing an Alpha Phi Alpha t-shirt taking out his trash at the garbage dumpster.

What were the odds that I would come outside of the leasing office to make a call at the exact moment an unknown fraternity brother would be wearing a fraternity shirt almost like a beacon of light walking across the parking lot where I was standing? Talk about being in the right place at the right time. After coming down to Florida with nothing, homeless and literally outside of one potential home and at the same time, caught a glimpse of someone who could possibly help provide another home option. He was like another "human angel" put along my path to help. Those were great odds so I couldn't hesitate and had to act now!

Nikki was in the middle of talking when I quickly said, "I'm going to have to call you right back."

Of course, me being a somewhat freshly new member of the fraternity, I rushed across the parking lot excited to go and introduce myself to another brother of the frat. His name was Brother Bresean Jenkins. As we started talking, I found out he had joined the local graduate chapter of the fraternity less than a year ago and was a local minister in the area starting a church. As we continued talking I found out that not only were we fraternity brothers but that we both attended HBCU's (Historically Black Colleges & Universities) and that we both were born and raised and from North Carolina. I told him I had graduated back in May from North Carolina Central University and he said, "Oh wow my little brother Kevin went to school there, did you know him?"

Surprisingly, I did. Being known for my not being able to control my facial expressions, I remember thinking to myself not to make a face as I recalled in that moment why he and I weren't on the best of terms due to a shady business transaction that was never resolved.

We stood there chatting for a while about the fraternity and how he had come to live in Florida. My curiosity got the best of me and so I felt compelled to ask, "How did Kevin become a member of our "rival" fraternity if you joined Alpha?" As he began talking about his brother I uncontrollably blurted out that he still owed me money from a graphic design project back in college. He laughed and immediately said that sounds about right, then started to tell me about the graduate Alpha Phi Alpha Chapter - Nu Eta Lambda and the brothers in the chapter.

I was instantly relieved because he could relate but also concerned that he knew his brother well enough to believe a story about him by a complete stranger. I told him about my current living situation and right there he made a phone call to one of the brothers working at the University of Florida, Brother Bryan "BPatt" Patterson. By the end of that phone call, Bresean told me I could crash at his place for the first week and BPatt said I could stay until I got on my feet and worked out my living arrangements. Just like that, I had a place to stay and a huge obstacle on this adventure was overcome because of fraternal brotherly love. I literally didn't know these guys beyond our connection through Alpha Phi Alpha but they were ready to welcome me into their homes. To me it felt like something higher was directing my path and connecting the dots by placing people in my life to build connections and relationships that could help me. I was out of the park but this journey was just getting started.

After talking with Bresean, I remember having a sense of relief and thinking things were lining up for me. I walked back to the leasing office and told them I would take the apartment but needed to push back my move-in date. Gainesville was a college town so as classes were starting, apartments had become less and less available. Thankfully, my apartment wouldn't be available for a few weeks so that gave me time to get some money together. I signed my lease and returned to the newspaper with a huge smile on my face looking like if Black Boy Joy was a person.

I felt comfortable with the decision to sign the lease on my first apartment on my own because it felt like I was supposed to be here. I had the car, I had the internship, I connected with a fraternity brother in a moment of despair who was letting me stay with him temporarily and secured an apartment all in the same day. It just felt like things were lining up. Like something bigger than me was ordering my steps and all I could do was follow.

Living with Bresean during that time was really interesting for me. I'd lived at home all five of my undergraduate years but had never been roommates with any except for my sister. My grandmother had limited space at her home and we were forced to room with each other until my sister finally left for college so I was accustomed to sharing a living space. He was gracious enough to provide food and a temporary residence until I got on my feet. Breasean had another roommate so space in this apartment was even more limited than my grandmother's home but we made due. I slept on the couch and was thankful because I could finally stretch my legs instead of sleeping cramped up inside a compact

Dodge Neon. He introduced me to more fraternity brothers in the area and I began to slowly build my Florida tribe.

Later that week, I decided to drive around to get acclimated with the Gainesville area while looking for a good Black-owned barbershop to continue the two haircuts a week regiment I had started back in college. I came across World Cuts on the eastside of town. Ironically, it was in the same shopping center as the only Food Lion grocery in the city. At that moment, I felt like it was meant to be. What were the odds that the grocery brand my sister had worked for was located next door to the first Black barbershop I saw? It had to be a sign. I wrote down the address so I could MapQuest it when I got back to the office and started to head back to work. As I was leaving the parking lot, I recall pulling up behind a dark blue two-door Hyundai Tiburon sitting at the stop sign. The driver was just sitting there, either they were lost or indecisive. Either way I needed them to keep it moving. Becoming more and more impatient with this driver just sitting there, I went to hit my car's horn to get him to move along. It dawned on me that I didn't have a working car horn so I just sat there in my feelings.

While trying to get the driver's attention by making eye contact in his rear-view mirror, I noticed this horizontal square shaped Alpha Phi Alpha Fraternity, Incorporated air freshener hanging from his rear-view mirror as clear as day. For some odd reason that I will never be able to explain , I distinctly remembered that particularly odd shaped air freshener with our fraternity's brand because just a year earlier when I was going through the process of becoming an Alpha, I had crossed the burning sands with a guy by the name of Jacqúin "Quin" Gilchrist from Davidson College back in North Carolina. Due to military duties, Quin was unable to cross with his chapter so he joined me and my line brothers from the Gamma Beta chapter and crossed with us as our extended line brother. Through the fraternity process, Quin and I clicked instantly and became friends but after we crossed he went back to his chapter outside of Charlotte, NC and I went back to mine in Durham.

When I noticed the air freshener hanging from the car's rear-view mirror, I threw my arm out of the window to throw up the "Phi" hand sign to signal that I was frat. The driver immediately did the same while looking back from the driver-side mirror. I caught a glimpse of his face and said to myself, "Nah, it couldn't be..." and I put my car in park and quickly hopped out shouting at the driver, "Quin?"

He got out of the car and to my surprise it was him. He was in town starting law school at the University of Florida Levin College of Law and was also looking for a barbershop just as I was. By then, we were holding up the parking lot but I didn't care. I had a friend from back home that I actually knew from North Carolina so those cars could wait. I went up to him and gave him the biggest hug as if it was my long, lost brother returning home. I told him I was in town for an internship with The Gainesville Sun that would later be a job with the Gainesville Guardian newspaper. Quin said he lived on the Eastside well technically in Rochelle, FL just outside of East Gainesville.

We exchanged contact information and made sure we stayed in touch. It was my first week in Gainesville and I had already made contact with a local frat from back home, found a barbershop and a place to stay, and the skies were the limit from there.

The next week, I arrived that Monday morning ready to meet both Witzel and Kratzer who were freshly back to work from vacation. I was the first person in the office so when Witzel walked in he was confused as to who I was. I wasn't sure if he stopped in his tracks because he was shocked I was there or if he had forgotten about me completely. After spending my first week checking Facebook and walking around the newsroom, I realized that besides the late-night press workers, custodians or the managing editor's secretary Joe who resembled a fluffy, big-hearted George Jefferson, I was the only other Black man in the newsroom. With about ninety eight of the newspaper's interns coming from the University of Florida only a few blocks away, I think it's safe to say that he might have assumed I was "someone" else. He and I talked briefly as we went over what my duties would be as a photo intern, you know typical first day stuff.

After getting all the technicalities out of the way, he asked me how my first week had gone. I caught him up on how I spent my first week of checking Facebook and trying to figure out a place to stay because I left North Carolina blindly without one. I told him about meeting my frat brother and getting an apartment not too far from the newspaper.

He looked at me surprised and said, "Why did you do that?" I said, "Do what?"

And he asked me to repeat myself and so I did. I repeated myself from the beginning that I had met a fraternity brother while looking for a place to stay and secured an apartment so I would have a place to stay when I started working for The Gainesville Guardian after the ten-weeks like he had said.

He looked me right in my face and said, "I never told you that."

For a second, I thought he was joking. I mean we clearly talked about this before I packed up everything I had in my Dodge Neon and drove over eight hours to be here.

I asked him to repeat that for me and he said, "Yeah, I never told you that."

I said, "When I was in North Carolina you said after the ten-weeks I would be working for the Guardian but you couldn't tell me how much I would be making yet. I needed a place to stay so I got an apartment."

He said, "Are you kidding me?", then asked how long my lease was. I told him it was a one-year lease, this was my very first apartment so I assumed most leases were for just one year. He told me he would have to talk with Human Resources at the New York Times Regional Media Group to see if they wanted to pay for me to break my lease. I was slightly discouraged, thinking I had misheard what he told me before coming down to Florida. There was nothing I could do but wait and see what they said.

Witzel asked if there was anything else that happened while he was gone and I told him I met Charlotte the editor of The Gainesville Guardian newspaper and our meeting wasn't the most pleasant. He asked how so and I told him, "Well her exact words were, you know you belong to me now," and how uncomfortable that brief interaction was.

He told me not to worry and that there were changes happening with the Guardian newspaper because the executive editor and publisher didn't like the direction the newspaper was going in. I sat in on a meeting about the direction of the newspaper and initially the focus was on the more stereotypical perspective of early 2000's Black culture in Florida such as customized early 1970's Chevy donks, shiny car rims and the latest fashion trends instead of the diverse interests, news, talent, occupations, and lifestyles of Black residents on Gainesville's Eastside.

To me, that might have worked for a section in my college newspaper, The Campus Echo but not in Gainesville where the community was predominantly white and black residents that made up a small portion of the population. It wasn't my place to say anything so I just sat in that meeting keeping my thoughts and opinions to myself.

On Aug 21st, NYT regional newspaper the Herald-Tribune published an article that the Gainesville Sun launched the weekly newspaper, The Gainesville Guardian announcing Charlotte as editor. Three days later, on August 24th, 2005, The Gainesville Sun newspaper published an article announcing Rob Oglesby and Doris Chandler, the newspaper's first black journalist, as the co-editors of The Gainesville Guardian newspaper and myself along with Cleveland Tinker, Colleen Flannery, and Teresa Southern were announced as the Guardian news staff.

After that, not a word was ever mentioned about Charlotte. It was as if she was replaced overnight without a word and we were all to act like business as usual. Within a week, the Human Resources department of the NY Times Regional Media Group had followed up with Witzel after he had informed them I had started my internship two months late and that I had got myself a one year lease. Christine Bence, who I had stayed in touch with after the journalism institute and helped me with getting my internship, had contacted me and Witzel and to both of our surprise the status of my internship had been upgraded. Instead of paying to break my lease, my internship was extended from ten weeks to a year with the NY Times Regional Media Group paying the newspaper my weekly stipend after the ten week period.

I was so proud to call home to tell my mother the good news. When I got home to my apartment I went to my bedroom, got on my knees and went to God in prayer just to thank him for making a way. I knew it was only Him who put these "Human Angels" in my path at the right time to help when I needed it most. I felt like I was meant for something more, like this was where I was meant to be. Over the next few months, I would mail home copies of articles with my photos. When I would call home, my mom would give me words of encouragement and tell me things at home were good. She never let me know just how bad she was struggling to maintain the house and take care of my grandmother. By the time I returned home for NCCU homecoming, my grandmother's Dementia had gotten worse and my mother was let go from her administrative job at a local doctor's office and couldn't afford to maintain the house with the excessive amount of repairs needed to bring the house to adequate living conditions. Within a year, with the lack of money coming in, we lost the house and my mother made the tough decision to put my grandmother into a nursing home. I remember sitting in the nursing home manager's office with my mother watching her sign the admission papers, admitting my grandmother. Her hands were shaking and had tears coming down her face.

I hugged her afterwards and she held me tightly saying to me, "I hope she forgives me for this."

Right then I knew this was one of the hardest decisions my mother ever had to make. I began to cry but tried to be strong for my mother. I felt so helpless knowing that things had reached this point and I wasn't in any position to help out financially. I was just an intern at a newspaper several states away and every penny I made went towards my apartment.

The year went by so fast. Although I had started my internship in August of the previous year, classes at the University of Florida were coming to an end and a fresh stock of interns would be coming to the paper for summer internships just as I had the year before.

Technically, I had more than a month left in my internship and wasn't sure if they were going to go the full year or cut my internship so the new interns could start.

Unfortunately, there was no room in The Gainesville Guardian's budget to hire an actual photographer and I hadn't lined up another internship after this was over so I was all out of options. I couldn't go home because I didn't have a home anymore to go home to. My mother was living in a one bedroom apartment with barely enough room for one person so I knew two was definitely a crowd. In my final days as an intern there was so much racing through my mind. What would I do if this didn't work out? How would I go back "home" to nothing? Did I work hard enough? Am I a failure? These were just some of the thousand thoughts immediately shooting across my mind at the same time.

I tried to remain as quiet as possible around the office in hopes that the photo directors Rob Witzel and Brian Kratzer would forget my internship was coming to an end and just let me stay. Around the end of July that year I was called to the newspaper office after a photo assignment. I walked into the photo office, and both Witzel and Kratzer were there. I remember thinking to myself, *this is it? Damn, I wasn't ready for this yet. This couldn't be over.*

They told me to pull up a chair. As I sat down, I realized it was just the three of us in the office as Kratzer reached across to close the door. I remember wondering what they were going to say. As I nervously sat there on the end of my seat, I noticed they both were sitting there, kind of leaning back with their arms behind their heads. Just as calm and casually relaxed while a full set of fireworks of emotions were running around inside my mind. As Kratzer began the conversation, he started to tell me how great it had been having me around as an intern. Witzel sat there comfortably reclining in his chair with his arms still behind his head, with not a single expression on his face. Right then I knew this was it. There was a long period of silence in the room with not a word from Kratzer or Witzel who was still sitting there with this blank stare on his face.

As I sat there fighting back the tears, I started wondering if everything I had done in the past year led me to this particular moment? Then it finally hit me, I didn't have a plan. I couldn't go home without a job. My mom had already endured so much and I refused to become a financial burden on her.

Kratzer looked over at Witzel and with a slight smirk turned back to me and said, "Since you're not an intern anymore, we would like to offer you a photography position at the Sun." In my mind, Kratzer had become Tyra Banks and all I could hear was, "You are no longer in the running to be America's Next Top Photojournalist, please pack your things and leave." Still fighting back tears, I thanked both of them for the opportunity when it dawned on me what he had said. At that moment, I couldn't hold them back any longer as tears poured from my eyes with overwhelming relief. I couldn't believe I did it.

I had just accomplished something major. Not only had I secured my first job after graduating but I was making history. The Gainesville Sun, which was founded in July 1876, hired a young black boy from Durham, North Carolina as the first black Staff Photographer precisely two hundred and thirty years after the newspaper was founded. Not only was I making history, I broke the cycle of complacency within my family. I wasn't only the First to graduate from college and the first to move out on my own and now the first black photographer of both The Gainesville Sun and The Gainesville Guardian Newspapers.

I stepped out on a limb, followed by dreams, let God lead me and found success because I wasn't afraid to take a leap of faith. When everything was questioning me, I prayed harder and never folded. I found success through the connections I made with the people who were out along my path in this journey. Each and every person were "Human Angels" who came at the right time to help me at the right moment when I needed help.

In one year, I moved to Florida with nothing, was homeless and had to learn how to be an adult quickly. As doors were literally being opened for me, I overcame each and every situation because of the connections I had made.

I'm reminded of the a quote from the Bible that I have heard time and time again throughout my life, "God is faithful, and he will not let you be tested beyond your strength but with your testing he will also provide the way out so that you may be able to endure it" (1 Corinthians 10:13 NASB). I believe I'm a living testament to that biblical verse. I was tested and through my courage, faith and persistence I prevailed. It was nothing but God guarding me while guiding my steps along the way. Through my faith, I knew he wasn't going to let me fail. This journey showed me why it is important to stay connected to people. To stay connected to your faith whatever that may be, and to stay committed to your passion, your dreams and your goals. I live my dreams every single day because of the connections I have made. Because I took a leap of faith and let the connections I made help jumpstart my journey to live in my passion.

It's true that sometimes people do come into your life for a reason or a season. You never know how the people you have connected with could just be the right person at the right moment at the right time to help shape your tomorrow and elevate you along your own journey to living out your passion, goals and your dreams.

"This journey showed me why it is important to stay connected to people. To stay connected to your faith whatever that may be, and to stay committed to your passion, your dreams and your goals. "

AARON DAYE

5

SAY YES!
MANIFEST MORE IN YOUR LIFE

"He who is not courageous enough to take
risks will accomplish nothing in life."
—Muhammad Ali

ARNISHA T. JOHNSON

DEDICATION

To God, for blessing me to become a mother to my amazing children
To my husband, for always pushing me to never lose myself
To my mom, for teaching me valuable lessons that's shaped my life forever
To my children, mama will always manifest for you. I love you all!

When I was a young girl, my mom struggled with being present at every event (plays, concerts, awards ceremonies) my siblings and I had, let alone prioritize her needs and desires. This was devastating to see her being pulled in every direction with little to no support and with our fathers barely in the picture, she could only do her best. I recall my mom telling me about a time when I was two years old, I caught chicken pox and with no one to help her, she ended up dropping out of college to support me. Whenever she shared that story, it would come with a bit of sadness because in reality she put her dreams and desires on hold to make sure I was taken care of. This would become the pattern for all of my siblings growing up.

After having a total of four children, my mom worked more often to do her best for all of us and when my needs became more financially demanding, I moved in with my grandmother. It was the best decision my mom could have made for me because she knew that my grandmother could provide for me and my needs more than she could. Sometimes, I didn't see it like that, especially when my mom couldn't make it to every concert I had or show I was in. After a while, I figured with now three mouths to feed and needing to take care of everything herself, my mother didn't need to explain the reason why she couldn't be present.

I thought moving with my grandmother made things easier for my mom, but I returned home only to witness her still doing the same thing. As the oldest, I felt it was my duty to step up and help her with cleaning, cooking, taking care of my siblings, and even getting a job afterschool. If I lended my hand, maybe she would have more time to spend with us and do more family things. Unfortunately, that wasn't the case. She didn't want me working to help, so she pushed herself harder to do it all. I even remember asking her if I could get a job at fourteen and her response was, 'You're too young. You don't need to focus on that. Focus on school. Do better than me.'

I followed instructions, focused on my grades and school, and also got a job. I knew I couldn't just let her do it all by herself. I didn't have children, so I could focus my energy in supporting our family and my mom in return could focus more on our family. My goals became clear: go as far as I can in school, work hard to earn my own money, and focus on building a better life that didn't include struggling, especially with children. It was during this time that my work ethic developed, the hope for my mom to be more present with our family became stronger, and the notion of making 'better' choices sat in the forefront of every decision I made moving forward. Your childhood truly shapes your mindset, your journey, and your decision making.

Once I became a college student and then a graduate, I followed my heart and went straight into teaching. After two years of classroom teaching, a Business Degree and passion for Education, I knew I wanted a career that would marry both experience and passion. I met the love of my life at a time when I was most alone. I had dated a few people and knew that the next relationship I entered would be one that I would spend the rest of my life with. The courtship wouldn't feel rushed or forced, but organic and authentic. The night we met all started with a 911 call, as he was the responding officer that arrived at the building where my friend's car was broken into. We exchanged information after the investigation and it went from there. Over the course of two years of dating, he proposed and I was welcomed into his and his son's heart. James and I were looking to relocate because where we were living didn't have as much potential for us to flourish professionally. During the job hunt, I claimed aloud that I would indeed find a company that would allow me to hone my skills in Business and Education.

The power in speaking your desires aloud has a funny way of showing up in reality. Less than two months later, I landed that job and began working with a brand new company as an Assistant Director of a tutoring and enrichment learning center - the best of both my passions. This was the first confirmed instance where I started to believe in the power of the law of attraction and manifestation.

At my new job, all of the employees were either fresh out of college or young married couples. Just like me, yet oddly enough, no one in the US database for the company had any children, nor desired to start a family. We would chatter about our relationships and of course the children's question came up: "Are you guys thinking about having children?"

"Not at this moment." That was the typical response, especially from the married couples.

For me, that wasn't the case. As a newly married couple, my husband and I knew we wanted to expand our family. My husband had a desire to have more kids and I was ready to start a family of my own. Two months after we got married, we found out we were expecting and were excited and nervous. Gratefully, during my pregnancy I was promoted to Director and became the first and only U.S. maternity employee. The Company even built their U.S. maternity benefits package around me. This sounded great from the outside looking in, but what my job failed to understand was that rolling all of my earned PTO and sick days into this package meant returning to work with no financial security to take time off for my health or my baby's. Others at work couldn't comprehend what that meant in the long run. They weren't planning to have children anytime soon. I needed time with my newborn and needed my fullest earning potential at my job.

I didn't want to make the decision to drop my passion because I didn't have a choice; I knew I had to 'make better decisions' than my mother did. Deciding what to do after the benefits ended was the hardest choice I was facing at this moment. If I returned to work, that would mean missing my child's first moments and if I choose to leave my job, that would mean losing my income. There are moments in your life that once they're gone, you can never get them back. I knew I had to do something. So, I declared aloud that whatever decision I make would in fact be the best decision for me **and** for my family. Speaking my desires aloud had a way of becoming reality so I knew I could make it happen again, making sure I followed up with taking action. I researched stay at home moms, heard stories of how they enjoyed being available to attend appointments, games, piano lessons, karate classes, playdates, and even midday ice cream socials, as well as being able to work at their own pace. They expressed their joys of being present and how it impacted the lives of their children, no matter the age. Even after I took action and researched, I found myself almost living in my manifestation, my 'best' decision. I wanted that freedom of being a thriving Stay At Home Mom (SAHM). I dreamt of the flexibility I would have being present with my daughter. I spent so much time dreaming, thinking, and feeling the moments I would have when I was home fully with my daughter, that I'd built up the courage to take my leap of faith and do what was best for me and my family.

I was sitting across from the company's supervisor who negotiated my maternity package, my learning center's regional director who'd had a conversation with me regarding my desires to have a work/life balance within motherhood, and the company's lead trainer who interviewed me for the company. This trainer was also one I personally confided in with my worries and stressors. Before I acted on what would've felt like an impulse, I wanted to meet with my supervisors to weigh out all of my options. I'd hoped my dream company, which valued children and families, would find a way to create a work/life balance that would benefit both my needs as a mother and the needs of the company. For two hours, I expressed my love for being a first-time mother, shared my enjoyment gained from working with the company and families, expressed the time I needed to attend appointments and the secure space I needed for pumping, and requested flexibility from the company to support my needs as a mother and an employee.

After all of those efforts, they countered with questions of how I would make it work and what solutions could I come up with. It seemed that the more I requested support from my company, the more uneasy I felt about resuming my employment. It was as if they didn't want to work with me to make this balance beneficial for both parties. I'd really hoped this option would've worked best for my family and I, but replaying what was happening in that moment just became too much for me to handle. So I took a break and went to the bathroom where I called my husband and told him I wouldn't return to a place of business where the value I had of being a mother would be diminished because of the needs of a business. It seemed that right then and there, the best decision I was already contemplating, dreaming of, even manifesting, was about to happen.

I'll admit, I was scared as hell for the decision I was about to make, but I knew what I wanted and had to be confident and faithful in my next steps. This is what it feels like when you take a leap of faith and step into your manifestation. I walked back into the room, uncertain and hopeful of what would come next, and told the staff present I was grateful for the opportunity but I was quitting today. Truthfully, I expected some form of shock or negotiation from the management staff present at the table; I mean I had worked there for almost two years.

Instead, their responses were, "Okay."

While I wanted to show my reaction of disbelief, I replaced that with full confidence that what I desired most - being a SAHM - God had waiting for me. I asked for the nearest computer to type my resignation letter, printed it out and signed, even thanked them for the lessons I learned because I knew they would be transferred somewhere later in my life.

Some of the other staff members asked me what was next. With a confident smile on my face, I replied, "I'm not sure, but I know whatever it is, it's going to be amazing!"

When you decide to quit and people ask you, 'What's next?', never shy away from the confidence that your desires will carry you into your next adventure. Simply reply, "Something amazing," and walk into your purpose.

At that moment, I stepped into my manifestation, saying yes to what I wanted and what I felt was best. I sat in the car that day for what seemed like hours, just replaying what happened in my head. I cried tears of joy. Then, I prayed, laughed, and shouted to the rooftops! I did it! I manifested what I wanted more out of life and this situation. I wanted more freedom, more flexibility, more time with my daughter and I was going for it.

That night, my husband hugged me and said, "Finally!" It was as if he knew that was the best decision I had made, and indeed it was. He'd witnessed how much I poured into work before my daughter, including the time I sacrificed away from him to manage my team and center. It was exhausting and not fair to him. I sadly conditioned myself to think that working all the time was okay, willing to give up my desires and be unhappy just to say I had a job. (Sounds familiar right)

Here I was, without kids, working as hard as my mom did with children. Had I kept it up when my daughter was born, I would've made the same decision as my mother did, instead of a better one. It's best to do what's best for you especially when you know it's time and it was certainly my time. I couldn't believe what I'd done. Quitting! I felt so free. Free to make more decisions that made me happy and my family happy. Free to manifest more in all areas of my life. I now possessed the power to command the things I wanted more of. My sacrificial story wouldn't come with slight regret and sadness, but with confidence and manifestation that the decisions I made moving forward would bring me peace.

The power you wield when you say yes to what you desire truly can change your life forever. This gave me clarity on what I was meant to do next.

*

Two years after I quit, manifesting more of what I wanted and saying yes to what I desired became a part of my everyday lifestyle, snowballing into a lifelong journey of peace, clarity, purpose, freedom, and more. I shared my story so much with other entrepreneurs who found themselves where I once was, stuck between no other choice and saying yes to your desires. Sharing inspired me to become a Certified Law of Attraction Life Coach - guiding others on how to attract and manifest more in every area of their lives. The skills and lessons I learned from my dream job, the passion for education and business, showed up at this very moment, commanding me to start my own life coaching and business consulting company. Realizing the very thing I quit, positioned me to coach MomPreneurs and others on how to manifest more, reframe their mindset from employee to becoming CEO of themselves, their family, and their business, speaking professionally, and encouraging many people to become their best selves by saying yes to their wants and desires.

I own my own time, am present with my daughter and earn an honest living running my business like a CEO. I create my own work/life balance, where I'm in control of my time and provide the flexibility needed to teach my daughter and run my business efficiently and effectively. Manifesting doesn't just stop here. There's more I want in life and I know there's more for you too.

If you find yourself deciding whether or not you should stay in your current situation or miss moments you can't get back, when you're ready to manifest on more in your life, declare and state aloud what you truly want. Say it with conviction, with belief, that you deserve that better decision. Take action, including research, to learn more about all of your options because you indeed do have options. Be open to dreaming, thinking, and even living in your declaration and desire. Know that the current state you leave behind provides the necessary skills for your journey ahead. When it's time and you're feeling scared, uncertain, and even hopeful, take that leap of faith and step into your manifestation knowing that your next steps will be "amazing!" You possess the power to say YES to what you desire, and deserve. Manifest more!

"Be open to dreaming, thinking, and even living in your declaration and desire. Know that the current state you leave behind provides the necessary skills for your journey ahead. "

ARNISHA T. JOHNSON

6

BUILDING WINGS

"The need for change bulldozed a road
down the center of my mind."
—Maya Angelou

KRYSTAL ELZY

DEDICATION

To my son who loves me unconditionally. I would be lost without
you.
I loved you first.
To my brother and sisters for accepting me for who I am.
To my mother for always, always, being there no matter what.
To my best friend who has been my entire rock and who always
saw my potential when I couldn't see it myself.
I love you all so very much!

The first true memory of my father was when I was about five years old. He was lying in a hospital bed with a beautiful smile on his face. My mom put me in the bed with him and we talked. He was looking at my hand because I had a little wart on it. He was telling my mom what to use on it to get rid of it. The next memory of him was the day of his funeral. I was looking up at my mom and I asked her why she was crying. She looked down at me and told me my daddy was dead. That was thirty five years ago. My father was only twenty-nine years old when he died from cirrhosis of the liver. At the age of five I couldn't process what death was, but I knew that day I was very sad.

At the time of my father's death, it was just my older brother and I. We were inseparable. I remember following him around all the time wanting to do everything he did. If he played with legos, so did I. If he was watching cartoons, so was I. If he walked around with his shirt off, I did as well. I just had to be in his presence. I felt safe when he was around. I admired my big brother. He was my first best friend. It was just the two of us for a while but then came my two beautiful younger sisters. I have a middle sister who is four years younger than me and lives here in Jacksonville. She is the most caring and thoughtful person I know. And crazy hilarious! There's never a dull moment when she and I are together. My baby sister who is seven years younger lives back home in Pensacola, Fl. One thing I can say about my baby sister is she is going to have your back! No matter the situation, she is going to show up ready for whatever. This is my family, me, my brother, my two younger sisters and Mom. I was the only sibling that grew up without a father. I can honestly say, I never had anyone in my life that I could call Dad and I believe this has caused a lot of emotional issues in my life such as dysfunctional relationship decisions, trust issues and self worth.

Growing up in a single parent home had some tough moments. We didn't have a lot growing up but my Mom worked hard to make sure she provided the necessities for us. She worked so much and sometimes had to leave us home alone. Since I was the oldest girl, I had to grow up fast and take on more responsibilities to help my mom. She taught me how to be strong and independent, and that no matter how rough things may seem, I still had to be mentally strong to keep pushing through life's challenges.

My mom would always tell me I was ahead of my time. I believed she said this because I was more mature than most girls at my age. Being the oldest girl, I learned at a very young age to be independent. I was cooking meals, cleaning the house and combing hair at a very young age. Growing up, I've seen so much and been through so much such as domestic and sexual abuse and caused me to build barriers and walls to protect myself. It was hard for me to trust people or to open up to anyone. I bottled up so much pain, anger and resentment, to the point it consumed me and that's who I'd become. This angry, rebellious, sad, young girl.

Once I entered high school, I pretty much had a normal teenage life. I joined the band, the track team and had a part time job. I hung out with friends, had boyfriends, you know, just a normal teenage life. But in the summer of 1998 I met who would become my on and off boyfriend for the next twenty years, through a mutual friend. He was parked at his cousin's house sitting in his maroon colored boxed Chevy. For me it was love at first sight. I knew this guy would be my boyfriend. We exchanged phone numbers and the rest was history.

He was going into his freshman year in college and I was going into my junior year in high school. While he was away at school, we would talk everyday for hours at a time just talking about any and everything. I remember him coming home for the winter break. He drove to my Mom's house in his brother's black Mustang and that night we talked for hours into the early hours of the morning. It was something about him that made me feel I could trust him, and I felt protected. I was able to let all my walls down with him. And at that very moment, I knew in my heart that he would change my life. That night we made our relationship official.

We dated up to my senior year in high school and spent a lot of our time together and ended things right before my high school graduation. I don't remember the reason, but I remember being extremely sad. My mom saw how depressed and unambious I was. She didn't want me to stay in Pensacola and do nothing. So she and my brother talked me into moving to Gainesville, FL and going to the community college there. I would be close to my brother who was attending the University of Florida. But I'd been so intent on staying home in Pensacola, FL, going to the local community college and being with my boyfriend. That had been my whole plan. But since we were no longer together, I decided to go. I moved to Gainesville and attended Santa Fe Community College from 2000-2002 and it was one of the best decisions I could have made.

College was probably the best time of my life. I met many people from so many parts of the world. Since I went to the community college, I stayed off campus in an apartment with three other girls. This was my very first time living on my own and I adapted fairly quickly because of me being so independent as a young girl. Although I didn't have a car, I learned the bus system very well. My brother was already living in Gainesville two years prior so he would show me around the area. I got an on campus job, joined the Black Student Union and went to some amazing fraternity and sorority parties. I was living my best young adult life. College really brought out the social side in me. It taught me how to be my own self, speak my own mind, and stand up for what I believed in. At one of the student union meetings they were giving away tickets to one of the biggest on campus parties. In order to win these tickets you had to stand up in front of the audience and tell them who you would want to have a conversation with if you had the opportunity to go back in time and why? One person said Martin Luther King. Another person said Malcom X. I stood up slowly, voice shaking and trembling. I was fidgeting with my hands and so nervous because everyone was staring at me and I simply said, "I would like to have a conversation with my Dad. " I would tell him that I needed him to protect me and I need him to be there when times get hard.". That was all I said. At the end of the meeting when it was time to announce the winner of the tickets, I thought it would be the guy who said Malcom X, but they called my name. I couldn't believe it. That was the very first time I ever spoke in front of a crowd.

Although I didn't attend the university, I met some very influential people there. One of those people was my brother's girlfriend at the time. She was absolutely beautiful and so classy. She would always tell me to hold my head up as high as I could no matter what I may be going through mentally, and to never let it show on the outside. She also would tell me to always be a lady in public. Carry yourself with class and dignity wherever you go! Although I was enjoying college life and living on my own, my grades were suffering tremendously to the point of no return. So I dropped out and moved back home. I was disappointed in myself, but going to college and living on my own taught me how to be financially independent, it gave me the opportunity to explore my true self and develop a sense of being comfortable in my own company, and it taught me how to set healthy boundaries. Which I still practice to this very day.

When I moved back to Pensacola, I had plans to enroll into the university back home but those plans never happened. Instead I moved back home with my mom and enrolled in a vocational training program where I received a medical assistant diploma. Me and my ex still kept in touch while I was in college so when I moved back home we rekindled our relationship and decided to move in together. This seemed like the logical thing to do. During the two years we lived together, I was completely dependent on him for everything. He was a great provider. I still didn't have a car when I moved back home so he bought a car for me to use to get to work. He was extremely money-minded and took care of the major expenses in our apartment. He was there for me in ways my family wasn't. If I needed money, I could go to him for it and he would provide it along with the lecture on saving and being more financially responsible.

We had some good moments while living together and at other moments he made me feel like an irresponsible child. We argued mostly about him being gone or out late and having his friends over all the time. I thought moving in together would get us closer to marriage, but it did the opposite. There was no compromise, we both just lived two different types of views on life. I felt like he wanted me to be a wife without actually making me his wife. He had the typical family dynamic. He grew up in a two parent household filled with support, security and financial stability. I came from a single parent home that barely expressed love and affection. While I yearned for that love and security, he wanted support. But I was mentally incapable of giving him that support he needed. And after two years of living together with each other and realizing that it wasn't a good decision, we decided not to renew our lease and end our relationship once again.

We went through so many break ups; more than I can count. Each break up I would lose a piece of myself. I would feel more and more worthless. My self-esteem was diminished. I'd lost the drive to want to further my education or do anything that really made me happy. I had completely lost myself to a toxic relationship. I solely depended on him for happiness and purpose. I believe that because I didn't have a father figure in my life, I relied on him to fill that void. I relied on him to protect me. I was very insecure with myself and it caused so many problems in our relationship.

I became so obsessed with trying to make it work because I was so afraid of being alone. I was afraid of losing my protection. Even if it cost me my sanity and happiness, I was determined to make this work. I knew our relationship wasn't healthy and it needed to end, but I couldn't face my demons alone. I needed him in my life because I felt he made them all disappear. Instead it created more drawbacks in our relations. Even though he was there for me when I had no one else, he lacked emotional support; and that really affected my self-worth. When I suffered from depression and anxiety he would dismiss it as if it was nothing at all. And that would hurt me to the core. But I still needed him in my life.

We continued this rollercoaster of a relationship for several more years. I was in such a low-spirited state of mind that it would alter my behavior if I wasn't with him. My family would tell me I was miserable, that I looked sad all the time, that I was mean and hateful. And they were absolutely correct. I would lash out on them sometimes for no apparent reason at all. I felt like no matter how much I poured into our relationship I was losing so much of myself. I just wanted to receive the same type of love I was pouring out. I know he cared for me and did love me ,but it wasn't the same love I had for him. Needless to say, we ended up breaking up again.

Between 2006 -2007, I was living my life again. I got a one bedroom apartment, started working at a better paying job, found a church home and sang on the praise and worship team, and enrolled in school full time. I began hanging out with friends again and even started dating! I can honestly say I was happy. Me and my mother's relationship had gotten better. I was doing things I absolutely loved. But because Pensacola was such a small city, I would run into my ex from time to time. Sometimes it would be good moments, other times I would be acting a total fool if I saw him with another female. Even though I was living my best life and dating this amazing guy at the time, seeing my ex with another female would feel like a sharp piercing knife in my heart. The guy I was seeing at the time knew I still had feelings for my ex and that's why it never really got serious. Honestly, it would never have gotten serious as long as I was still in love with my ex. So of course we ended it. Yes, you guessed it! My ex and I started seeing each other again. We were back on the rollercoaster.

It was January 2008, and I was sitting in my gynecologist's office complaining of sharp pains in my right side. See when I was about nineteen years old I was diagnosed with PCOS and was told by three different doctors that I wouldn't be able to conceive because of this issue. I would develop these large cysts on my ovaries that prevented me from having a menstrual cycle and when they would get a certain size, they would rupture and cause the most excruciating pain ever. So to prevent this from happening, I would either have to take birth control for the rest of my reproductive life to shrink the cyst or have my ovaries removed. I chose to take birth control.

When my doctor came in to see me, she delivered some unbelievable news. She said, "Well Krystal, most likely you do have a large cyst on your right ovary, but you're also pregnant."

Yeah, I wasn't buying it. I didn't believe her. In fact, I told her she had the wrong chart and began to spell my first and last name to her. She said, " Miss Elzy, I know who you are and how to spell your name. You are pregnant!"

I couldn't believe this. For seven years I believed I would never be able to have a baby. The first person I called was my mom. No matter the status of mine and my mother's relationship, I knew she was the only one I needed at that moment. When she answered the phone I burst into tears and told her I was pregnant. Because of the status of our relationship, it took me two days to tell my ex. I was afraid of his reaction since we weren't actually back together. I knew it wasn't going to be as welcoming as my mom's reaction, and it wasn't. In fact we got into an argument about whether I should keep the baby or not. To me this was my miracle and I led with my heart.

I can honestly say, I had a good pregnancy. Absolutely no morning sickness, I didn't have any strange cravings, as long as it was food; I was good. I worked out up to about six months of my pregnancy and then I just got too big to do anything but walk slowly. I signed up for lamaze classes, breastfeeding classes, and any other parenting class I could find. I enjoyed everything about my pregnancy. Before my son was born, my mom and I agreed it would be a good idea for me to move back home so I could have help with the baby. I am so thankful she was there because I don't know if I could have done it alone. On August 18th 2008, I delivered an 8lb plus baby boy! I know he would change my life forever.

Anyone who knows me knows my son is my entire life. I was overjoyed with happiness. The love and joy this baby brought to me was more than I could take in. It didn't matter to me if my ex and I weren't together, because my son filled all my voids. Being a mother gave me exactly what I was missing all my life. My son brought me unconditional love.

When my son was about six months, we moved out of my mom's into a two bedroom apartment. Living with my mom for the support was great, but boy oh boy was I ready to leave! We couldn't get along! She had something to say about everything I was doing as a mother. I wouldn't let anyone pick up my son without them washing their hands first, you couldn't hold him for long, you couldn't kiss his face, you couldn't feed him anything other than milk. I was very particular about my son. I was a first time mom and I wanted to do this my way. I was a very hands-on mother because I know I didn't want my son to have to go through some of the things I went through as a kid. I showed my son love and affection, I expressed love to him. My ex and I could provide our son with more than I had growing up and that was very important to me.

Regardless of our relationship, I made sure he had any and every opportunity to be in our son's life. The more time he spent with our son, the more time we spent together as a family and that's what we wanted for our son; for him to grow up with both his parents together. So we decided to try one more time and raise our son together as a family.

Things were going well, I graduated from college in 2010 with an Associate degree in business, the next year I got on with an amazing company and although we lived in separate homes, we were raising our son as a family like we planned. We would spend some time at his home and he would spend time at mine. We did family things together such as movies, dinner, and spending holidays together.

Seeing him as a father was amazing and brought the greatest joy to my life. He was very hands on and supportive and this made me want more out of our relationship. I wanted marriage. He would tell me that marriage was just a piece of paper and he didn't want to marry me. Knowing that never sat well with me and it really bothered me because now I felt I wasn't good enough for him to marry and he was just going through the motions with me because we had a son together and so many years of history together. It made me look at our relationship differently and I began to question everything about myself. Was I not worth being married to? Was I not good enough for marriage? What was I doing wrong for him to not want to marry me?

Our relationship started to go down that slippery slope again. The arguing was getting so much worse than before.

We would argue about the past lies that were told, the infidelities that we just couldn't get past. I wanted to make things right so I agreed to go to counseling. But all that did was reveal how toxic we were to each other. The relationship had become so bad that I went into a deep depression. There were times I wouldn't go to work. I would stay in bed all day while my son was at daycare or school. Some days I would miss taking him to school. I developed anxiety so bad that I would have to leave work some days. I didn't understand why he couldn't see the struggle. I was going through depression. This deep sadness lasted for years. I felt trapped. I felt defeated. I felt broken to the point of no repair. I was going through the motions of self destruction. I nearly lost my job. I remember lying in bed saying to myself if I don't snap out of this, I am going to lose it all. I was trapped in my own mind and I knew that the only way I was going to become myself again was to get out of this relationship. I had to dig deep and use the strength I was using to hold on to him and use it to let go. I had to take my life back. With the support of my family, friends and getting more counseling, I decided the only thing to stop this vicious cycle of a toxic relationship was to leave Pensacola altogether.

Leaving Pensacola was my plan, but I didn't know where I wanted to go at first. I have family in San Antonio, Tx so that was an option, but it was just too far. I still wanted to be close enough where I could come home often so that my son could see his father. Then one day I received a phone call from my very close cousin who is like a mother to me. She told me she had a career opportunity in Jacksonville, FL and that if she got the promotion, I needed to come with her. This was my chance! This was my way out! It was far enough to start a new life and get away from this toxic relationship but it was close enough to still come home often. I didn't think twice about it. When she called me back with the news that she got the promotion, I started preparing for the move. Looked for a house and a job. Once we found a home and I was called back about a job I applied for, I told my son's father what I was planning; but he had plans of his own. I wasn't prepared for what was about to happen in my life.

One evening after work and picking up our son, I went to my mom's house. I remember just sitting out in the car for a few minutes before going in. Someone came out of nowhere and tapped on my window. "Are you Krystal Elzy?"

I nodded and he slipped a thick envelope through the small crack of my window and said, "You have been served," and walked away. I didn't even see where this man came from or when he left. I knew exactly what was in that thick envelope. I had been served with a court order to deny me from relocating. The next day, I immediately contacted a lawyer. He looked over the documents, asked me a few questions. Then told me to continue with my move. And that's exactly what I did. I continued on with my plans to move to Jacksonville until it was time for our court date. My son and I moved to Jacksonville January of 2018 to start our new lives. I started my new job and he started at his new school. We would find something new and different to do every weekend.

Before our court date I had a very intimate conversation with my son. I wanted to let him know what was going on. Anyone who knows me, knows that the relationship with my son is absolutely the most beautiful thing. This was no average ten-year-old. My son's comprehension of things was profound. I wanted him to know there was a possibility that we may have to move back to Pensacola. I remember my son saying, "But Mom, is that what you want?"

I said, "No, I don't want to go back but it's not my choice anymore".

He said, "But you're happy in Jacksonville and I haven't seen you cry since we moved to Jacksonville."

The thought of having to move back home put me right back in that depression state. I was so afraid of going back into "the dark place" again. That place was scary. I couldn't breathe in that place. I couldn't think in that place. I couldn't heal in that place. I was emotionally dead in that place. I prayed and prayed and prayed for God to just give me a sign to help me make the right decision.

The day of our court date, I had this feeling that things weren't going to turn out how I wanted them to. I tried to mentally prepare myself for the worst news ever, but all I could think about was how would I make it if I had to move back home to Pensacola? After hours in the judge's chambers, he finally made his decision. He denied my relocation request and told me I would have to move back to Pensacola. This was the most devastating news in my life. When it was time to tell my son we were moving back to Pensacola, I couldn't hold back my tears in front of him and he began to cry with me. He just held me and kept telling me it was going to be okay. "We're going to be okay Mom."

"What was I going to do? I kept asking myself over and over again. What was I going to do Lord? I can't go back home. I won't make it mentally."

I sat in the middle of my bed crying uncontrollably asking myself, "What will people think of me as a mother? What will my son think of me?"

Anyone that knows me knows I love my son more than anything on this earth. We have a bond like no other. How will I make it in life without my son being with me every day? I continued to pray to God for answers. But all I felt was fear. That night before going to bed, I sat down with my son and asked him how he felt about him staying in Pensacola without me.

My son looked at me with tears in his eyes and said, "Mom, we're going to be okay, besides this will give me time to bond with Dad and I'll get to live in two different cities." I knew then that God had given me my answer. The next day my grandmother called and said to me, "Krystal, I was thinking about you and I want you to know that boy is going to be okay. Now you are a good mother, and good mothers have to make tough decisions sometimes. You're going to be alright."

I have now been in Jacksonville, Fl for three years. The decision to stay here is something I think about every single day. Being away from my son for long periods of time is still difficult. Some days I question myself, "Why am I here and not in Pensacola with my son?"

But moving here has changed my life in so many ways. It was like I'd gone through the molting stages of my life. When a bird is shedding their feathers to grow new ones. I was shedding so many layers of depression, sadness, and fear to build a new life filled with peace, self love, and growth. I was able to really discover myself again and reveal the true authenticity in myself. I absolutely love the person I am becoming. Once I decided to do what was best for me, I discovered what peace really felt like. I know what real happiness and joy feels like! Despite what people may have said or thought, they will never ever understand what I was fighting against. No one will ever understand the unfathomable emotions I was dealing with daily. I had to drown out all the noise and negativity of others by doing exactly what I wanted regardless. When you have walked through darkness for so many years, there is nothing anyone can do or say to take you back to that place again.

This move has shown me the power and strength I had within myself all along. I have accomplished things that I thought I would never do. In October 2020, I completed my Bachelor's degree in Human Resource Management and received the promotions I worked so hard towards. I've met some amazing people that continue to encourage me daily. I have overcome so much fear and doubt in myself because I decided to take that leap of faith. But most importantly, the relationship with my son continues to be prodigious no matter the distance. We have a bond that can never be broken. My son is now thirteen, and has been the most supportive and influential person in my life through this journey. He is the reason I have made it this far. He is my person and I will continue to do great things because he believes in me. When I have those moments of doubt, I remind myself of everything I have been through and it gives me the subtle reminder that I have power to overcome anything.

She took a leap and built her wings on the way down

~unknown~

" *I had to drown out all the noise and negativity of others by doing exactly what I wanted. When you have walked through darkness for so many years, there is nothing anyone can do or say to take you back to that place again.*

KRYSTAL ELZY

IIII

COURAGE

**"History has shown us that courage
can be contagious, and hope can take
on a life of its own. "**

~MICHELLE OBAMA

7

UNBOTHERED & FREE

"Let your enemies become your foot stools, your test become your testimonies and your messes become your messages."
— Zane

WADELENE "MS. WEALTH UP" CHARLES

DEDICATION

This chapter is dedicated to the influential women in my life, starting with my amazing mother Marie T Charles. I literally would not be here without you. You've taught me how to see the good in everyone and how not to be quick to cancel people even when they may have an opposing point of view. You've taught me the power of self control and consistency. Thank you!

Little did I know, the woman I called Mom would become the new Wadelene Charles. The woman that nurtured me, cared for me, taught me how to clean, and how to cook. Not only that, but she brought me into her business at fifteen years-old and taught me the basics of bookkeeping and taxes. The woman that ignited my passion for the world of finance. A woman that contributed greatly to the woman I am today, caused my world to come tumbling down before me.

This is not a story about my real mother. This is a story about a woman that was like a mother to me. A second mother, my blood sister. Yes --my own sister. We were provided the sustenance of life from the very same bosom. Me and my sister were like two peas in a pod. Where she went, I'd follow. She would pick me and my brother up almost every weekend from our mother's house and expose us to so many different things, an entire world outside of the confinement of our strict Haitian parent household. See, my parents were older Haitian immigrants that didn't know the language too well, so when I was home I was stuck in the house doing chores, homework or reading. I was a shy kid so I didn't have many friends and the very few friends I did have, my parents wouldn't allow me to travel to their homes.

My sister was one of our few hopes of actually doing different activities outside of school. My sister took me to my first concert, my first club event, my first trip outside of the country and helped me get my first car; the list goes on. I looked up to her immensely. She was simply amazing, she was my role model. She was headstrong, resilient, a fighter, and a business owner. And let me tell you. Baby was bringing in almost a million dollars a year and was married with two beautiful children at the time. She was the epitome of a strong, beautiful, black woman and I had great admiration for her.

Before I go ahead and jump the gun here, let me start from the beginning. My sister had recently moved back in with my parents after being fired from numerous jobs. Shortly thereafter, my father took her to enroll in a community college course for Accounting. She then landed a job as a Contractor working for the city in their Accounting department. I remember her coming home one day from work. That particular day, she called me into her bedroom where she had a desk set up with her work computer. She said, "Hey, Wadelene. Let me teach you how to organize this company's books. You need to learn a new skill."

I've always been a quick learner, have always loved numbers, and have always been a very analytical person, so I picked it up in no time. And I loved doing the bookkeeping work because I got to help her, you know. At that time, it wasn't the enjoyment in the task I loved most, it was being able to accomplish something with my sister. She was counting on me, so I delivered and frankly the tasks were fairly easy. I was essentially doing bookkeeping for the city, so I was super excited about that as well.

Learning the trades of bookkeeping and tax eventually led to her quitting her job and opening up her own practice, which grew rapidly. She opened multiple locations, we started taking trips, and we even went to Haiti a couple of times. I was a young, teenage girl living like what I envisioned the life of a successful business woman to be. I was learning all I could about taxes, bookkeeping, finances, the works. So just to give you a clearer picture: I was in middle school, the president of the student government, treasurer of the Key Club, and on the A-B Honor Roll every year. I had it going on!

I was the ideal student. But on top of that, I would leave school and go straight to work around four thirty nearly every weekday -- that was, if I wasn't already preoccupied with my presidential and other leadership duties. And I must remind you, that was just in middle school at the time when I started that job. I would get a ride or walk, go to the office and start working on clients' books and/or taxes. I'd always looked older than my age, so there weren't too many questions from the clients. I was fifteen years-old looking like I was about eighteen or nineteen.

So the clients didn't really care. They just thought, "Oh, you know, the adorable secretary girl is taking my information. It's fine." But little did they know, a whole fifteen-year-old was doing their taxes. And this fact alone was really cool to me.

Eventually, I went off to high school and studied Bookkeeping. I went to a technical magnet high school in which grades nine and ten, would function as a typical high school, but in eleventh and twelfth grade, we would enter into our predetermined technical program. My technical program was Accounting, rightfully so. Why not continue with something that I already know? So I studied accounting and loved it because I would be out of school by two pm and in the office by two-thirty, three o'clock if the city bus or my rides would arrive in time. Sometimes, especially during tax season, I wouldn't leave the office until about midnight. One o'clock in the morning, I'd be getting home. I'm sure there were labor laws against this.

Although I enjoyed interacting with people and helping them with their finances and taxes, it was tiresome and tremendous amounts of work. On the other hand, I felt great because I was making money while helping my sister and her clients make even more money. She was giving me anywhere between one hundred and fifty dollars to three hundred a week and I thought I was balling y'all. No Wizard Kelly.

I was like, "Girl. You started out making fifty dollars a week at fifteen. And now you makin' hundreds? Oh, you big ballin'!"

You couldn't tell me nothin'! That was me up until the Fall of 2010.

Now, this next part was one of the most pivotal moments of my life. It was the middle of tax season. Mid-March. We were literally up to our eyeballs in tax returns and other documents that needed to be filed. We needed all hands on deck. It was me, my sister, her husband, our brother, and the secretary. My sister's husband had just come back with the Chinese food and we were famished, so we all retreated to the break room. We're all just chatting away and my sister suddenly says to my brother, "You know what, Wadner, you're such a headstrong guy. I see you owning your own business one day. I can see you going off and being great." And in that same moment, she turned to me and the words she dared utter to her little sister, "Wadelene, you could never be a business owner. I just don't see it for you."

I was at a complete loss for words. One of my greatest role models told me "I couldn't" and my heart absolutely sank. I could hear the thump of my heart falling out of my chest and hitting the plate full of shrimp-fried rice that sat just below my trembling chin. I could feel the very same meal starting to come up from the depths of my stomach. The woman I admired so greatly, that I looked up to so much, had just told me I wasn't good enough. At that moment, that's exactly how I felt. That I wasn't good enough. Me. She didn't see my ability to excel or to build and grow an empire of my own. That infuriated me but more than that, it broke my heart. I sat there perplexed. I was completely silent for the remainder of the night.

I recall watching the clock until it was time for me to leave that Godforsaken place. I remember going home that night and as I trudged closer and closer to my bedroom, I could feel my eyes getting heavier and heavier as tears trickled down my face mercilessly until the waterworks became full-blown waterfalls. The next day I went into the office still a little taken aback from the previous day, I didn't have that same fire. The fire that was ignited in me began to fizzle out. I spoke nothing of the event that occurred that night until many years later.

While continuing to work for my sister, I made the decision to learn all I could from her company. I continued to pick her brain about how the business ran and different tax laws. I forgave her because I had to in order to move forward. Although the words she spoke to me that terrible night affected me, I began to bury those hurtful words so I could continue to be mentored and grow with the help of my sister. I knew high school graduation was nearing and after that moment I would take all that I'd learned and run off to college to start building my own empire. She went off to open a retail store and I helped manage the day to day tasks at the offices.

A little over a year later, I was off to college to soar on to greater things. I jumped into positions of leadership as a young teen because even though I was a nervous and shy girl, I aspired for more in life. I had dreams and goals and I wasn't going to stop until I achieved them. And at that moment years ago, I made a decision that I was going to prove her wrong. I was that shy girl that was going to achieve all that I had aspired for despite her lack of belief in me. I saw the future God had prepared for me and that was my biggest motivational factor. No matter what may come my way or what my sister may say or perceive of me, I was going to be ten toes down.

This next event was one of the catalysts that showed me that my mission was greater than I could ever imagine. It was bigger than just me. It was an event that shook my entire world.

I went off to the University of North Florida where I studied Accounting and Finance. The first in my family (distant cousins included) to attend and graduate college. Upon graduation, I landed a job in corporate Accounting, working for a fortune five hundred company making $45,000 plus bonuses annually at entry-level. I felt great about what I was able to achieve thus far. But one day, on a late Tuesday morning, I received the most heart-pounding phone call of my life.

It was a typical workday: I was reconciling the monthly transactions to consolidate the month-end financial statements of my assigned accounts. My work phone began to ring and the caller ID read, "Lobby Security". I was a bit taken off guard because the security desk rarely ever called. I answered the phone and a woman from the security desk downstairs was on the other end explaining that some government officials were there to speak with me.

I remember being beyond nervous. As I exited the elevator and turned the corner, two agents dressed in space grey suits approached me each with one hand reaching out for a handshake and the other hand displaying their badges. They spoke in what seemed to be in unison, "Hello, Ms. Charles, we are with the Federal Bureau of Investigation."

I responded in pure confusion, "The FBI?"

One of the suited men responded, "Yes, we would like to ask you a few questions."

Now, I thought my sister telling me I wasn't good enough to run a business was bad. *This* was an entirely new ball game. *Why was the FBI here? What could I have possibly done?*

The other suited man interrupted my thoughts.

"We are here to discuss your sister. She's under investigation with our agency for fraudulent activities and we just want to ask you a few questions."

I retreated back to my thoughts. I was utterly confused.

I knew it was my sister, but what did that have to do with me? Why were they here? At my job?

This was supposed to be a safe position in Corporate America. It was a fortune five hundred company for goodness sake.

Yet, there they stood, looming over me like duplicates of the treacherous Michael Myers.

Interrupted again by a monotone, "Why don't you have a seat, Ms. Charles?" He pointed to the section of plush upholstery armchairs in the lobby of my workplace.

I returned to reality and stumbled into the closest chair my body could find. They opened a manila folder. Inside was a picture of my driver's license. But it wasn't me on the license. It was the image of my sister.

See, at that moment, I remembered when I went to get my passport picture taken and my sister said, "Don't smile because if you smile, it'll be hard for them to identify you."

I replied saying, "Oh, that's weird, okay, I'm not gonna smile." After the picture came out, we joked about how much we resembled one another when I didn't smile. This memory was what triggered my next thought. Oh my gosh, my sister had stolen my identity. What had started out as an insignificant sibling joke had turned into absolute betrayal. And now, FBI agents were confronting me at my place of work. They continued on and told me they recognized this was my name and my identification, but not my picture.

They also showed me various bank accounts that had been opened using my forged signature and they all had overdrawn balances. My eyes bulged out of my head as they presented the verified documents before me.

I was stunned. I didn't know what to say or do.

As I examined the papers in front of me, one of the agents asked me, "Did you know about this?"

I confirmed I was unaware of the mischief that was done using my identification and this was completely new to me. How could the woman I trusted so much--the woman that told me if anything were to happen to her that I would be the only one that she would trust to care for her children--the woman that I mistakenly called, "Mom" because I felt so comfortable and safe with her?

How could she put me in harm's way to the point where I was now sitting in the lobby of my workplace with two representatives from the FBI?

Oh my gosh, I worked so hard.

I went off to college, the first person in my family to do so.

Graduated with two degrees at that, landed a job in Corporate America, started planning out the potential launch of my own accounting firm the following Fall, and then boom. I was now the victim of identity theft by my own sister.

How did this happen? Why me? Was my life over?

I had these bank accounts in my name with major debts and I didn't know what to say.

She was my sister.

I recall one official saying, "Hey, we understand you are a victim of identity theft and we understand you didn't know about this. We just wanted to make sure that you are aware. We're going to move forward with the case against your sister." Then I signed a few documents and they were gone as quickly as they had come.

The minutes felt like hours as I made the longest journey back to my desk.

I sat there in complete silence, staring at the blank screen in front of me until hours later, I saw my coworkers packing up to go home. I followed behind them, only physically present as I was still trying to process everything that had taken place earlier that day. I just couldn't believe it.

Not only was I not good enough in her eyes to start my own business, but she had stolen my identity. Till this very day, I have never felt so manipulated and betrayed in my life. She had been using my identity to open fraudulent accounts for years while appearing to still be the same loving and generous sister I had known all of my life. In moments such as these where someone has betrayed you or taken advantage of you, it's important that you remember only light can chase out darkness. When we seem to be surrounded by devastation and sadness, we must seek out hope and love. Life is already hard, but just like at this moment, I had to eventually remind myself of it's beauties and have faith that all things worked together for my good. I let my faith guide me and remind me that there were better days to come.

It took years to close out all of those bank accounts and to speak with the credit bureaus and insurance agencies to undo the havoc she'd placed in my life. There were accounts with thousands of dollars of overdrawn amounts, tickets, and credit card accounts in my name unknowingly. I remember going to the Community First branch on my university campus with a classmate and the banker stating I was unable to open any account with their bank. I was humiliated. The financial debris she had maliciously engineered had impacted every part of my existence.

My relationship with my sister took a drastic turn. We are no longer close friends, but continue to remain cordial at family affairs. And for whatever reasons my sister felt like she had to steal my identity and hurt me to get ahead, I have adopted that into my own cause. With forgiveness, you learn to use another's shortcomings and inflictions to find healing and live out a greater and more fulfilling life. When you hold on to past hurts and sufferings, it prevents you from allowing the light to come in and shine through because you are too busy holding on to the darkness. My ultimate desire is to provide financial solutions to individuals so they won't be tempted to stoop so low as to rob someone else of their future in order to feel like they are getting ahead.

My company's (Grand Reve Financial) motto is turning dreams into reality starting with financial success. I have come to realize that some people tend to do these heinous acts because of their financial incapability. People steal, cheat, end marriages, hurt or even kill due to problems revolving around money. I've forgiven my sister and adopted these moments into my mission. Use those hurtful moments to fuel your purpose and passions, not hold you back and fill you with agony or resentment.

I will never forget all I have learned from my sister and what those moments have taught me. They are a part of me and contributed to the woman I am today. I have gained tons of experience and insight.

I don't resent her, nor do I loathe her as most people might if they were in my shoes. However, my resiliency made it possible for me to continue to make progress in spite of her.

This alone shows me I'm destined for greatness. And the same can hold true for you. Let it go and live your best life; you deserve it. You deserve to live out the beautiful life you've envisioned for yourself. You just have to forgive and allow yourself to do just that. Regardless of what may happen, you have to be Ten Toes Down for your mission, your purpose, and your Best Life.

My favorite quote is, "I didn't come this far to get this far." I actually have it hanging in my bedroom. My best friend made me an image of this quote a few years ago. I look at it all the time, almost every day, as a constant reminder that although I have gone through so much, and am still going through different challenges and experiences, that I didn't come this far to come this far.

I didn't get my Bachelor's degree just to give up at the first sign of an obstacle. Not at the first sign of my own sister not believing in me, not when I experienced identity theft, and not even when I was denied by multiple banks and financial institutions. No, I didn't come this far to come this far.

I say all of this to say, I have a purpose to fulfill. To fix financial insecurities within my community. And I will continue to do just that because I didn't come this far to only come this far. It's a part of my purpose to help myself, my family, and my community achieve their dreams starting with financial success.

If there is one message that I would like for you all to take away from this situation, it is that no matter what may come your way, stay resilient and always remember your "why". If that means you have to hang up a motivational quote in your room to remind you to keep pushing like myself then, do just that. Maybe it means opening up about your wants and needs or asking for help. Whatever it may be, stay Ten Toes Down because you didn't come this far to just come this far.

I guess I can't be upset.
I never let you get to know the real me
Because I was too busy smiling & laughing.
I sat and I listened to you talk about you
Then when you were done, I asked you to tell me more
So I didn't have to reveal my inner thoughts.
The sadness that lurks behind my smile
The tears in my laughter
The pain in my eyes.
I guess I'm not upset.
Not at you at least, but at myself
For always hiding the most honest parts of me.
I'm mad at myself for always shying away from revealing…
well,
Me.
Let me be free
Unwavered and unbothered.
I am beautiful in all ways even in my darkness.
Let me be free!

- Ms. Wealth Up
Wadelene Charles

" *When you hold on to past hurts and sufferings, it prevents you from allowing the light to come in and shine through because you are too busy holding on to the darkness.*

WADELENE "MS. WEALTH UP" CHARLES

8
READY!

"Character is power."
—Booker T. Washington

CHRIS SLADE

DEDICATION

I dedicate this Chapter to my God, My Family, and Myself.
Trials will come and go. With these 3 entities.
I will build my wealth.

What's good everybody? So…to give you some perspective on this chapter, let me start off by saying I'm writing this while creating a PowerPoint presentation for my graduate school class in Educational leadership. I'm also simultaneously developing lesson plans for the Resource-Skills class I teach for grades Kindergarten through Fifth at an Elementary School, and it's only the second week of school. I'm also in a meeting right now on an app planning a huge Met Gala event for my city's media and entrepreneurs, that is run through my events/entertainment company.

After this I have to knock out some flyers for a weekly event I run through my second company with a partnership that does pretty well in the city. Shit, I almost forgot I also have to get started writing my second album, which I'm a week behind with, and surprisingly a little nervous to begin. That process is always tough to start, but that's another story for another time.

And after all that's done (and sometimes during) I have to be a husband to an extraordinarily beautiful woman, and a father to two amazingly gorgeous daughters who we had in 2019 and 2020. Right. We had them little girls back to fucking back. In a pandemic. Shit is real.

Now at this point maybe you're asking yourself why? Why does this dude do all that? Or why does this matter? Hell, I don't know. Maybe it's the cards I was dealt. But all this helps to explain why anybody can manifest a positive destiny, especially when it seems like things won't happen. Truthfully everything started happening for me at the same time, and I just landed here. What's dope about managing everything is I actually don't mind the work it takes to maintain it all. In fact, I think it's part of a bigger purpose that will lead me to a dope ass future. I just have to do the work, and do it well. Or so I imagine. It takes a lot to "make it" in the world.

Let's start at the beginning. I'm originally from Jacksonville, Florida. The Northside, Dunn Avenue to be exact, although I spent most of my time with my grandma on Moncrief Road. But we're not going back to my childhood, that's too far. I just wanted to rep my hood. Let's start a couple years after college, around 2008. See back then, I used to be the guy most people clowned. Probably for good reason because truthfully I didn't know whether I was coming or going. For a long time, I honestly didn't think I was going to be shit. I flunked out of FAMU my last year, which was fucking embarrassing, and had to make it all back up just to graduate. Even though I messed up, and the experience was horrible, it motivated me in a sense because I felt I had an opportunity that most niggas never get.

Or so I thought. I say that because when I and most of my friends returned home, we didn't do shit. I mean we literally sat around and smoked weed all day, for hours and hours, only getting up to go home and then hitting each other up the next day to do it all over again. Bummiest shit ever.

I used to fall asleep at a moment's notice and wake up in empty rooms. I don't know how I didn't end up really fucked up now I think about it. Anyway, I think a light bulb went on after my second time getting pinched for weed by the police. You heard right. The second time. We won't go into any details, let's just say I got lucky. Ironically, I was on my way to make a pop (sell weed) and go smoke when it happened. I think that's what may have turned on the bulb.

For some odd reason (not odd at all), I realized I was fucking up. I had to be like twenty four years old. No job, no money, no girl, no priorities. About to go smoke weed with people who always clowned me and talked about me. Then it hit me. I was that guy. I was the guy everybody clowned to feel better. I was the dude nobody expected to do anything, and part of their day was making sure I knew it. I used to treat people like that, and now I was the person. Shit messed with me for about a week or two until I decided to switch up. It's crazy because in hindsight I couldn't tell you at what point things actually started to change. I just set my mind and all of a sudden it happened.

No. No. I'm lying. I know when it happened. I was staying with my homeboy, who is now the Godfather of my daughters. We had this apartment on Arlington Expressway in Jacksonville. My older brother and his partners were running a club night at the beach, and we went out there every Friday night. Apparently, somebody knew that because we got home that night to find our door kicked in. It was messed up too because that night we were coming back with girls to smoke and drink on an afterparty type vibe to find the door kicked all the way in. Like it wasn't there at all. So, there was no afterparty.

Instead my best friend and I got into a fight and he left the place seeing as I had to file a police report. Now, I won't go into full detail of the incident, just know they ransacked our place, and didn't take anything. I'm pretty sure you can do the math. Things got pretty awkward when the police came. The officer kept smelling everything (even though the whole apartment smelled like a pound), and asking me questions like "who I had a rivalry with", or "could somebody be targeting me in a beef," you know real "I can tell you're a drug dealer," type questions.

He ended up filing the report and I cancelled the lease and had to move in with my Grandma back on Moncrief Road. Depressed doesn't even begin to describe the feeling. My homeboy and I got back cool after some time, and for about a year and some change we just ran the streets. Hustling and doing call center jobs. In Jacksonville everybody has worked in a call center. It's kind of like a rite of passage here. Then the beginning of the decade hit. Once 2011 came around, it changed everything. So, 2011 was when I got into education. I had a degree in Psychology and couldn't do jack shit with it, so my mom (who just so happened to be a Principal) convinced me to go into education in order to save my life. Boom, just like that I became an elementary school P.E. Teacher. I wasn't too excited, but wasn't doing shit else and needed money. Shortly after, I met the woman who would become my wife while I was out Downtown one night. It was a party and I knew the majority of people there, but not her. We had seen each other here and there in the city, and had even met previously, but nothing came of it. So, I stepped to her at the function we were attending and she shot me down. Not in an ordinary "Boy bye," or "Chile please," kind of way though.

She told me if her cousin, who I was standing next to at the time, told me it was cool, she could give me her number. The catch here is her cousin had known me since the sixth grade, and they were very strong minded, assertive black women. So naturally the cousin asked if I was serious. I said yes, but it wasn't like other situations. She pulled me to the side and said, "Nigga you better be dead ass serious about this one, because I know you. If you don't have your shit together, don't even try."

Since I don't try to be in the business of wasting serious women's time, I took heed and explored the situation with a more mature attitude. To say the least, it worked out, but I will never forget to take the opportunity to appreciate it. Situations like mine don't happen often, if ever. I truly believe if not for that night, life would be completely different for me right now.

Ok, let's fast forward a bit. It's 2012. My now girlfriend and I decided to move in together. We got an apartment well above our means, and then I was laid off from my school. She had a great job in healthcare, but now it was back to being a bum for me. To add insult to injury, I decided to pursue a rap career and then attack the music industry full time...and get on unemployment. I even got a little buzz,. did some work for some labels and released some mixtapes. I performed at shows, met some major artists, and was really on my way (in my mind). But bills were piling and the reality of my woman leaving me and sending my ass back to Moncrief was beginning to settle in.

2014. After a long road of meetings, my rap performances, extra curricular activities that comes with this lifestyle such as bars, drugs, launch parties and video shoots, club appearances fights, beefs, and other bullshit, I decided to go down a different route. A famous person (I'm not name dropping) told me rap was just a part of the bigger picture. He asked me if all I could do was rap. That question set me on a course that put me in an Entourage-like (yeah, the HBO show) frame of my mind. I realized I wanted to start my own company. I didn't want to just be a rapper, I wanted to own the business that paid the rappers. And rap too, if I wanted. That mindset opened up a lot of lanes and opportunities that would soon turn into financial gains and successful outcomes.

But before that happens…I had to go through a little more bullshit.

In 2015 I decided to get back into education and direct myself into a different path by creating a company with three other friends of mine. This company had tasked itself with developing a market of entertainment for the African American young professional culture in Jacksonville, Florida. We started that by creating an annual event that was held at the beginning of the summer. This event had become well attended, but some of the group members didn't feel they were being paid enough from the business being done.

After the second year of the event we agreed to go our separate ways. The relationship ended in turmoil and things got worse as time went on. One of the members cut my partners and I out of the event and took the business for himself. He then legalized the company without the rest of the founders and made himself the CEO.

Having to regroup, I developed my own brand and set out to create an even bigger image for the market I had vision for. This sparked one of the business partners from the original group and myself to form a company that could represent our thought process in a more fitting way. We came up with a staple event in 2017 that represented African American culture to the fullest. We grew the event over the last five years and started partnering with other established groups to throw more events of the same nature.

Before you knew it, we were throwing two events a month and even whole weekends. We got into politics and began being staffed for political campaign advisement. We began throwing politically charged events for voting, local government, as well as state government with a growing reputation for controlling the urban young professional market in Jacksonville. Different well-known groups in the city were asking us to partner with them. Recognizable political figures, such as the Senator, started to acknowledge us for what we were doing in the community. We began utilizing venues such as museum rooftops for our staple event, and partnering with major venues to help get more attendees out to their establishment.

I also started another company totally by myself geared towards art, music, fashion, media, and city events that houses a weekly event that has been running for over a year now. Our name in the city has become fully recognizable as a leader in the market we help to create. And we are honestly just getting started...not too shabby.

Meanwhile I leveled myself up in education and started advancing myself in the world of the public-school system. I was elevated to Department Head of Social Studies at a middle school and implemented an entire program of Law Studies for seventh graders. I now have district specialists putting me up for higher roles and I'm having lunches with executive directors exploring paths for my future.

I'm being shopped for leadership roles in Charter schools and I was hired for the best position I have had in my whole career this year. I'm in graduate school for educational leadership and recently became a doctoral candidate with a 4.0 GPA. Shit's crazy. But like I said...we were just getting started.

Oh shit! The music. Yeah, so I'm rapping again too. I established a website with all my mixtapes, shot a video with some local legends, and released my first album on all media platforms. The album is based on the lives of the Black Panther

Volume 2: Defining Moments

"*Many things in business become a distraction once a certain amount of success swings your way. It's all about what you want in the end. I'm realizing and understanding these days that most people don't have an end game.*

CHRIS SLADE

09

A PIECE OF PEACE

THE ART OF SEEKING UNDERSTANDING, EXPRESSING GRATITUDE AND SETTING EXPECTATIONS

"Challenges are gifts that force us to search for a new center of gravity. Don't fight them. Just find a new way to stand."
—Oprah Winfrey

SIMONE "SAGE REEDS"

DEDICATION

Mom, this is for you. You are a beautiful woman and an incredible teacher. You always say God blessed you with the perfect child, and you're right. But do you know what God blessed me with? The perfect mother. I love you immensely!

Granny, you are the blueprint. I've learned so much about grace, love and kindness just from watching you. I'm convinced that the perfect grandmother exists because you exist. You love me in ways neither one of us can explain, and I love you even more. Thank you for everything. I love everything about you.

Auntie Portia, I love you, girl. Thank you for loving me like your own when you didn't have to. I've spent years watching and admiring you, and your heart is what I love the most. You are so gorgeous inside and out, and if I can be half the auntie you are, I've succeeded. I love you like money!

Sonler, I love you. Our love is sweet because we allow each other to just be. Thank you for seeing me, loving me and giving me space to explore my many layers.

Melynda, thank you for strong arming me into writing this chapter, love. Your belief in me encouraged me to believe in myself! I'll talk about you until the end of my time. Thank you for everything.

Lastly, for the person who seeks peace, know that the words in this chapter are a direct message from our creator to you. Read them, internalize them and trust your process. Peace is on the way, love.

It was a bright, cool August morning. That I remember. With her heavy hands (do all black parents have these?) and stern voice, Mom shook me awake. "Sweetie, wake up. Get up. Time for school."

With growing knots in my stomach, I walked into her bathroom, brushed my teeth and hopped into the shower. I walked to the other side of this new, huge and unfamiliar house to put my clothes on, and right before stepping into my new room, I spotted Granny in the hallway. I detoured into her arms.

"Mornin', Mona," she said, smiling.

"Good morning, Grandma."

"You ready fi school? Mek sure you hurry up so I can do your hair." Born and raised in Jamaica, Grandma (and my entire family) speaks fluent patois.

Feeling even more anxious, I went to my room, got my clothes on, felt very weird about not wearing a uniform for the first time in my life and pondered the same thoughts and questions over and over: *How far away is my new school? I can't believe I'm finally going to school in America. Will I have a locker? I'm going to miss grandma. Is American school different from Jamaican school? I love my mom, but I love Grandma too. I'll really miss her.*

Once I got dressed and gave myself one last look in the mirror, I ate breakfast, joined Mom and Granny in the living room and sat between granny's legs to get my forehead brushed, my neck jerked and my hair parted in two. She secured my parts with two scrunchies and two clips (one on each end), slicked down the few baby hairs I had and used her hands (and a little more time than usual) to smooth out the flyaways. She knew like I did that once the flyaways were

146

smoothed out and my hair was nice and slick, the moment she and I were absolutely dreading would soon arrive.

After the very last combing, I thanked Granny, got up, grabbed my backpack and walked into the laundry room which led to the garage door. As I put my shoes on, I kept my head down, and at that moment, the knots in my stomach grew into a rope that seemed to reach up to my tear ducts, squeeze them and cause them to release more tears than I thought I had. For the first time I could remember, I was now about to live away from my grandmother, her kisses, her meals, her healing hugs, her excitement as she greeted me from school each day and her love, grace and endless affection. To think that our moment of separation was finally here after spending so many years together sent the both of us swimming in tears as we hugged for the last time before her flight back to Jamaica and my first day of "American school."

Realizing that if she allowed us to, we'd hug and kiss until the end of time, Mom reminded me it was time to go. "Come, baby. I know you will miss Grandma, but we have to leave. You can't be late for your first day." Sobbing, we gave each other one last squeeze and one last kiss.

"I'll miss you, Mona," she said. "I love you."

"I'll miss you too, Grandma. I love you too. Have a safe flight," I responded as Mom and I walked to the car.

Looking back after every step, I waved and blew kisses until I was secure in the backseat and couldn't see her face anymore. Mom kissed her, told her she'd be back soon, hopped in the car and at just nine years old, I was off to my new school and our new life together.

At twenty six, Mom migrated to the U.S. for a change in scenery. Born and raised in Kingston, Jamaica, she is a natural-born hustler whose energy, ambitiousness and drive inspire everyone around her, especially me. She and her baby brother grew up in a tenement yard with my grandma, where they all shared a community bathroom, waited in line to use the kitchen and regularly fell asleep to gunshots. When she reminisces and we talk about her childhood, she's always grateful for everything she experienced, but at the same time, she'll always do what she has to do to stay away from ever living in poverty again.

As a young adult, she developed a fascination with America based on T.V. and what she heard from friends who lived there. It seemed pristine, luxurious and littered with opportunity—something Jamaica didn't seem to have at the time. Feeling stuck while working as a travel agent in a competitive, boring and toxic work environment (she once cussed out a co-worker over the intercom), she craved more out of life, her career and her surroundings. She wanted to roam pristine streets and enjoy the finer things in life, so in 1989 at the age of twenty six, she migrated to the "Land of the Free" to chase what she thought it had to offer: opportunity and peace in abundance.

When she finally arrived, Mom stayed with her aunt and cousins in Queens, New York. With a nice chunk in her savings, she didn't look for a job immediately. She wanted to enjoy this new American life without having to worry about work for a while. However, after hating the weather and expressing her feelings to one of her uncles, she decided to leave Queens after six months to live with him in Lauderhill, FL. He told her that South Florida was where it was at in terms of weather, and he invited her to stay with him and his family for however long she needed to. Once in South Florida, the weather was a lot better -- perfect actually -- but Mom quickly realized her dreams of roaming pristine streets and enjoying the finer things in life would require real work. Like hard, physical work. When she created her migration plan, she didn't take into account that most of the "opportunity" in America belonged to people with college degrees, a trade or people with the entrepreneurial spirit, not to immigrants like herself. When she came to this realization and checked her savings, which started to run low, Mom did what many immigrants do when they first migrate to America: elder care.

Living with her uncle was great. She loved him and his family, got treated very well and got to save. After a while, however, she longed for her own space, so in order to save more aggressively and move out faster, she got a second job as a home health aide, which is in the same field.

Now, you may be wondering why she didn't go back to Jamaica if clearly the American Dream wasn't dreamy after all. If she already had roots established back home, why not go back? Well, remember we're talking about my mom here --the natural-born hustler with crazy ambition and drive. She's also headstrong and stubborn. She wasn't going to give up on something she had started. She felt she owed it to herself to see it through, so she stayed and worked her ass off.

By thirty, she had a tiny one-bedroom apartment, a hoopty and two exhausting home-health aide jobs. Life became exhausting, routine and void of excitement, until one day, she got a call from one of her high-school boyfriends. With almost two decades of catching up to do, they spent the next few months talking, laughing and rekindling what they left in the past. He lived in London, so meeting up and spending time together was difficult, but they mailed current pictures of themselves to each other, spoke almost every day and began to really enjoy one another's company. As with many long distance relationships, however, the desire to see, touch and be in your boo's presence eventually becomes unbearable, and for Mom and her new boo, that became the case. They eventually decided on a date, he booked his flight, and in a few weeks, he flew to Lauderhill to visit my mom, and their reunion was everything they thought it would be. They enjoyed movie dates, amazing food and long-overdue kisses. They even talked about kids and imagined who they'd look like, who they'd act like and what their names would be.

Inevitably, during his visit, what they had imagined soon became their reality: Mom was pregnant! She was also not as established as she wanted to be, and her soon-to-be baby daddy was a British citizen who would soon return home. Would he consider moving to start a life with her?

When Mom told him about the pregnancy, what he responded with led her to cuss his ass out so bad that to this day, he still remembers every last word she said and every name she called him. She read him from top to bottom, A to Z. *How dare he not want kids right now? Didn't we talk about this? What does he mean he has to go back home? What the fuck did he mean he had somebody back home in London?* These are the thoughts she had as she realized that repeating our family's ancestral cycle of being a single mother was possibly in her future. It enraged her, saddened her and disappointed her. *How did she allow him to play her like this?*

For Mom, having an abortion was out of the picture. She was in her early thirties, her reproductive clock was ticking, and she'd always wanted kids. If she aborted this first one, she would probably never have kids again, and that's when she'd really hate him and possibly even hate herself. She decided to keep the baby.

So now here she was. Hurt and pregnant with a baby daddy who was back to living kid-free thousands of miles away. She had no money for any responsibility outside of herself, no time for much outside of work and no energy to do anything but sleep with the little free time she had. Add a baby to the mix, and she now had someone very expensive in her life to share her money, time and energy with.

Before getting pregnant, she always said she wanted to raise her children differently than she was raised. She didn't want them to watch her struggle, she didn't want to raise them in the hood, and she didn't want them to want anything she couldn't provide. Because of this, she hustled harder than ever before, deprived herself of the rest and nutrients she needed as a pregnant woman, and in September of 1994, she gave birth to her baby.

I was born with fluid in my lungs. With her body being used to hustling and bustling, Mom did extensive work around the house the day she went into labor, and when her water broke, she didn't notice. Being so focused on working, she went to the hospital hours after it broke, and during that time, I stayed in my amniotic fluid longer than I should have and began to intake the water. She always tells the story of the fear she felt when the hospital room got quiet.

She had a C-section, and when the doctors pulled me out, my eyes were closed, and I was quiet. She couldn't see over the separation sheet they put up between her upper and lower body, but she could feel. She felt the fear in the room. No one knew why I wasn't crying, but doctors spanked my butt and my feet until they heard something. Finally, after a little time, I screamed. When the nurse wiped me down and handed me to Mom, she said she first noticed my lips. They were his, and it was then that she realized that if she wanted to forget about him, she couldn't.

For the next two years of her life and the first two years of mine, serious postpartum depression kicked in for her. Again, she was broke, exhausted, angry, alone and most of all afraid of raising me in struggle the same way my grandma raised her. She had spoken to my father maybe once within those two years (in which she asked him for help but ended up cussing him out again), lost several jobs because she couldn't afford daycare (she took me to work, hid me and they found me every time) and had an almost non-existent support system (most of our family was in Jamaica, and the uncle who lived in Lauderhill did as much as he could).

Mom and Grandma have always been close, and one of my favorite things to do is listen to their conversations. To this day, when Grandma is in Jamaica and they talk on the phone, I sit beside Mom while she talks to her on speaker. When we're all together in person, I sit quietly in the room as they talk to each other. Not only do I love hearing them speak patois, but I also love their relationship dynamics. They grew up together, as Grandma got pregnant and had her when she was a teenager. They tell each other everything, throw shade at each other, gossip, laugh uncontrollably and always say, 'I love you.' It's so beautiful to witness. They really are each other's dawg.

As the pressure of being a single mother mounted during the second year of my life, Mom constantly vented to the one person who always listened and coached her: Grandma. She expressed how hard it was, how afraid she was and how she thought about giving up many times. During all their conversations, Grandma mainly listened and gave advice. One particular day, however, she came up with a solution: send Simone to live in Jamaica for a year so Mom could get on her feet.

At first, she refused and she refused quickly. It wouldn't feel right sending her only child away. Besides, she was headstrong as I mentioned, and when she started something, she had to see it through. Sending me to live with my grandma would have felt like quitting, and she had too much pride, so she thanked her for the offer, declined it, and we continued our life together. The suggestion, however, never left her mind.

Weeks/months later, Mom grew more exhausted by the minute. She now had a baby who walked, ate more, kept her on her feet and required a lot more of her money, time and energy. In her mind, there was no light at the end of the tunnel, and she felt she buried herself in a hole she couldn't get out of. Furthermore, when she sat down to really think about it, having a year to herself to hustle and create a better situation for my return didn't seem so bad after all. Grandma's offer began to look more and more attractive and after deep consideration, she took her up on it.

In 1996, at two years old, I moved to Spanish Town, Jamaica. Grandma flew to the states to pick me up. According to Mom, it was the hardest decision she ever had to make, but it was one of the most helpful things anyone had ever done for her.

Over that year, Grandma and I developed a bond that to this day, I can't fully explain. Though I don't remember anything from that time period, I know the attachment we have to each other today more than likely stems from back then. We were joined at the hip, she tells me, and when the year was almost over, she was so attached that she mustered up the courage to ask Mom to let me stay for another year. Mom, still working hard and appreciating her break, time and space to breathe, approved. I stayed.

I was now three years old, and during this new year, Grandma and I developed an ever deeper bond. She says I was a happy, loving and quiet baby, and she found it fun to be around me. Many grandparents love that they can return their grandkids once they get on their nerves. For Grandma, however, that wasn't the case. When year two came to an end, would you believe she asked for another year? Actually, would you believe that for five more years, she repeatedly asked for "renewals"? By the time I left Jamaica and moved back to the U.S., I was nine years old! Grandma kept me for a total of seven years, and at around four or five years old, memories began to form, and that's when I began to recall what life was like in Spanish Town.

When you look at the Caribbean on a map, Jamaica is a dot. You can literally drive from one side of the country to the opposite side in less than ten hours. That's like a drive from Miami to Pensacola! Point is, it's an extremely small country, and living there was a beautiful, yet completely different experience from living in the states. By the time I moved there, Grandma was well out the hood and was now living by herself in a spotless three bedroom, two bathroom home with a huge veranda and hair salon attached. In the U.S., we say front porch; In Jamaica, we say veranda.

As a child, I remember myself as being quiet and obedient. I didn't like loud things -- music, talking, laughing. I especially didn't like to hear people raise their voices, and being around arguments and animosity made me nervous. I was always described as 'the perfect child.' I listened to authority, followed all rules and did everything perfectly. With Spanish Town being so small, it gave me the quietness and peace my personality craved. I did a lot of reading (people are always shocked when I tell them I didn't see the Lion King until my mid twenties; I wasn't that fascinated with T.V. as a kid), a lot of observing, a lot of playing with my few neighborhood friends and a lot of laughing. It was actually annoying to people how often I laughed, but now we all crave laughter and joy. The irony!

I also did a lot of traveling--both to the U.S. and around Jamaica. Grandma made sure I visited Mom every summer; and my auntie (Mom's baby sister who was born more than a decade later than her) made sure I knew Jamaica. She has one son, and I remember her treating me like she had two children. Whatever she bought for him, she bought for me. Wherever she took him, she took me. My cousin and I went on lavish vacations to all of Jamaica's tourist spots, ate the best food and did every excursion you could think of. It was important to her that we not only knew our country, but that we enjoyed our childhood. She believed and still believes that life should be enjoyed and cherished, and that memories should be made. When I think of what it means to be the ideal auntie, I think of her. That's my girl!

You may be wondering about Mom during this time. What was she doing? How often did I see her in those eight years? Well, Grandma and I visited her every summer, and for all of my birthdays and Christmas, she visited Jamaica. I was so excited when she visited because I loved her presence. She was/is so beautiful and lively. It broke my heart every time she left, and as a child, I couldn't understand why. Why did everyone have their moms around all the time, but mine always had to leave? It's a question I held onto until we reunited for good.

When I turned nine, Grandma tried it one more time. After our seventh year together, we were inseparable, and it was harder than ever for her to let go since so much time had passed and so many memories had formed. She called my Mom to ask for the usual renewal when year seven came to an end, and to her surprise and disappointment, Mom declined. She realized that time was precious, and if she allowed more time to pass, there would be a possibility I'd resent her. Besides, she worked five jobs (at the same time) for several of those seven years to save $40,000, which she had put down on a brand new home near Jacksonville, FL. She wanted her baby back, and she wanted me back in time for her closing so we could move in and start our new life together. Grandma was devastated, but she agreed and understood, and in 2003, she packed up everything I had, and we flew to the U.S. for my second migration.

The Power of Understanding

Most people wonder and have asked me if I felt any resentment toward my mom. They can't understand how a parent of sound mind could send their child away and not fight for them for seven years. Who does that? And furthermore, they really can't understand how I was so welcoming of her fully coming back into my life after so many years. The truth is, I've never resented her. I had questions, yes. Of course. But I was never upset with her for her decision to allow so much time to pass between us. One of the things I love the most about myself is how understanding I am of most things. Not saying that I agree with most things; what I am saying is I understand most people's reasoning for doing most things. You don't have to agree with something to understand it. And when it came to my mom, I fully understood why she did it.

Here's the thing. I've realized having a sense of curiosity and a desire to seek understanding brings a lot of peace and helps me learn how to keep it moving. When we learn the ins and outs of a situation, chances are, we end up putting ourselves in the person's shoes, and we gain a sense of understanding. Many things are horrible and unforgivable both on the outside and when you dig deeper. Most things, however, *seem* horrible and unforgivable on the outside, but when we dig deeper, we learn the ins, the outs and all the variables, and this is where I think understanding and peace live, which ultimately helps us keep it moving. We all love talking about what we would and wouldn't do, what we could never do and what we would've done. But in all honesty, how do you know what you'd do? Unless you've been in that exact situation, it's important to note that we all have our own set of thoughts, feelings, values, emotions and DNA, and they all play a role in how we handle situations.

When I finally moved back with Mom and we formed our own little world, we had several conversations for years about the 'why' behind her absence. I wanted to know if she enjoyed her solitude more than being around me, and if she ever thought about the effect her absence had on me. She answered, telling me the story of how hard she had it financially, how she wasn't comfortable raising me in the struggle, and how the care I received from my grandma made it a lot easier to allow me to stay. This is when I developed a sense of understanding. I put myself in her shoes (considering her values and typical thought process), and it made sense to me why she made that decision year after year. Once I developed understanding, I was then led to peace. I also feel a sense of peace because I'm grateful. I'm grateful we came back into each other's life when she felt fully ready for motherhood. I'm also grateful she had a village because honestly, she could've raised me with no help while she worked her ass off and was always under pressure, but what kind of childhood would I have had? Though not conventional, her decision was for the best, which I see now, and there's a lot to be grateful for.

Note: If you truly can't understand the 'why' behind something, that's okay. Some things just don't make sense, and some things are unforgivable. Have grace with yourself. You'll find other ways to bring peace into your space.

Forgiveness + Gratitude = Peace

When I moved back to the U.S., Mom immediately made me a girl scout. I hated it. Today, I see the benefits of the organization, but back then, I didn't think it was fly or fun, and it wasn't what the 'it' girls at school were doing. However, we were both in a new city, she needed to meet people, and she wanted me to have friends outside of school, so whether I liked it or not, she thought it was good for the both of us. Every year, my girl scout group had a father-daughter dance that all the girls with present fathers looked forward to. For the girls with absent ones, there was a rent-a-father option.

I vividly remember my first and last time attending this dance. Both times were one in the same. Days before the dance, Mom and I went to Dillard's, picked out a dress, shoes, some ribbon for my hair and a little purse. She made sure I got my hair braided, wore tinted lip gloss (it had to be one that didn't look too much like grownup lipstick but one that gave me a little tease), sprayed a spritz of her child-appropriate perfume and wore deodorant. She drove me to the dance hall, walked me inside for registration, gave me a kiss on the forehead and told me to have a good time.

Once she left, I stood waiting for a few minutes as one of the leaders went to get my rental father. He was a super tall and warm, friendly white man who had three daughters of his own. When he came to the registration table, he smiled, held out his hand, asked for my name and took me to the dancefloor. Thankfully, he was sweet. He complimented my dress, my hair, my shoes, and we slow danced to a few songs.

I enjoyed myself, and it was cool until I looked around at people's faces. All I saw were eyes staring and mouths moving. It then occurred to me that I was a little black girl dancing with a white man at a father-daughter dance. Clearly, when you put two and two together, you get that this man is not my father, especially since all three of his daughters were girls scouts, and everyone knew him and them. I hated that everyone could tell I was one of the girls with the absent father, and I felt the most embarrassed I'd ever felt at that point in my life. I was around eleven years old. That night, I went in the shower, cried my ass off and told Mom I never wanted to go back to a dance like that again. She cried with me, called my dad a few names to herself and told me I didn't have to worry about it—she'd never let me attend again if I didn't want to.

Up until that time, I'd only seen my father once (still have only seen him once). He still lived in London after all those years, and he flew to Jamaica when I was seven/eight to visit his mother and siblings. A few days before going back to London, he made a pit stop to see me at Grandma's, and I remember pulling up to her gate after school, flying the van door open and racing inside to see him. Because I wasn't surrounded by many men in my childhood, I was so fascinated by the idea of having my very own father. I couldn't believe it when I saw him, and I was so shocked and excited that I ran straight into his arms and cried. Whatever emotions little me had inside regarding his absence came pouring out. He hugged me, squeezed me, asked me a few questions about school, and for the rest of the evening, I stared at him as he talked to my grandma. I just couldn't believe it. This was my father.

Before I knew it, it was bedtime, and Grandma reminded me to say goodnight. When I was all showered up and powdered down, he hugged me, kissed me and told me to sleep well (which I didn't do). The next morning as I got ready for school, I saw his foot hanging off the bed in our guestroom, and I realized he stayed the night. I tried to be noisy, so he could wake up, but he was a deep sleeper like me, so I let him be. Once I was all ready to go, I took one last peek in the room, stared for a few seconds and rushed outside to the honking van at the gate. That was my first and last time ever seeing him in the flesh.

Since that time, he called occasionally when I lived with Grandma and when I lived with Mom, but our conversations were always brief and forced. I didn't know him, he didn't know me, and as I got older, I lost interest in building any type of relationship with him. I didn't see the point. Mom played both roles, my grandma played both roles, and my auntie played both roles. I didn't feel I was missing anything, so from seven/eight years old onward, I kept him out of mind.

In college, however, my feelings toward him changed, as I had a roommate whose way of life fascinated me and inspired me to rethink how I felt about our relationship. You ever met someone who inspires you by just being who they are? That was her. She was the most present person I had ever met. She had battles of course, but the way she handled them and moved on was something I had never seen before.

For example, one day after her car got repossessed, she seemed peaceful. Mind you, that same week, she lost financial aid. When I asked how she stayed so calm, she told me that shit happens and shit will always happen. How you react to it is the game changer, and for her, she chose calmness and peace. She then mentioned the book *The Four Agreements* and suggested I read it to understand what she meant. In no time, I bought it, quickly read it and decided after years of not speaking to him, it was time I reached out to my father.

In the book, the author talks about not taking things personally. He says, "Whatever happens around you, don't take it personally. Nothing other people do is because of you. It is because of themselves. All people live in their own dream, in their own mind; they are in a completely different world from the one we live in. When we take something personally, we make the assumption that they know what is in our world, and we try to impose our world on their world."

Inevitably, I started thinking about all the people in my life who I felt played me. Friends came to mind and exes came to mind, but at the forefront was him. I realized I took his absence personally. Deep down, all those years, I felt that

161

because he didn't call me or visit me, the problem must have been me. When I read the book, however, and I really understood what it meant not to take things personally, I realized that whatever he dealt with had absolutely nothing to do with me. He lived in his own world, had his own way of thinking and had his own journey that led him to make the decisions he made. After this epiphany, I felt so relieved and refreshed, and at that moment, I decided to call him—this time, from a place of love. I wanted him to know I was in a different place and that I wasn't upset with him.

I remember the day like it was yesterday. I had finished my classes around noon, came home to an empty dorm, called my auntie (his sister) to verify that the number I had for him was correct, and before I dialed his number, I took some deep ass breaths. I had no idea what to expect from the conversation. *Will he be excited to hear from me? Annoyed? What if it's awkward?* With my stomach in knots and my hands shaking, I got out of my head, took one last deep breath and dialed the number.

In his thick British accent, he answered. I asked if he was speaking, and he said yes.

"This is Simone, your daughter," I said.

"Wait. Did you say this is Simone, my daughter?" he asked.

"Yes, Simone," I answered, smiling. The excitement in his voice gave me so much hope.

He spent the next 30 or so seconds laughing, saying 'Wow!' and telling me what a pleasant surprise it was to hear from me. I could tell he was in awe. He then told me he thinks about me every day, he asked how I was doing, how Mom was doing and how the rest of the family was doing. We talked about college life, my plans after graduation, what he did for work and life in London. The conversation lasted probably 15 minutes, and before we hung up, we both promised to reach out more. We said we'd never allow so much time to pass ever again, and we even set a date for the next phone call. It all seemed so promising. When I hung up, I felt like a daddy's girl, though I had no reason to feel like that from one phone call, but I guess I was just so excited for what was in store for us. When my roommates got home shortly after, I stopped them at the front door to tell them the news, I called my best friend to tell her, and I called my mom to share how excited I was to finally have a relationship with my dad. It felt so surreal. In the back of my mind, however, I found it strange that he thought about me every day. How do you think about someone everyday and never call them?

On the day of our next phone date, he called on time. We talked for about an hour and ended the conversation by setting a date for the next call. In between our designated call days, I made sure I was glued to my phone just in case he missed talking to me so much that he couldn't wait for our call days. To my surprise, he could always wait. And actually, after a short while, he began to either call late or miss our dates altogether. In no time, I began doing most of the calling, where sometimes he answered, and sometimes he didn't. When he did, he'd either say he'd call me back (which he didn't) or he'd sound annoyed, making it obvious that he didn't want to talk. This is when I got pissed, had several breakdowns, ignored everyone and stayed cooped up in my room (I didn't want anyone to know I got played).

What the hell is so important that makes him so busy that he can't call his only child? How does he not feel relieved that his child—whom he didn't and doesn't take care of—has no resentment toward him? How could he not jump at the opportunity to mend our relationship like most absentee parents would? I truly couldn't understand his attitude and his lack of care, and instead of trying to reason things out on my own, I decided to ask him, the source. I called him one day after class, asked all of the above questions and shared exactly how angry, led on and hurt I felt. What he responded with was shocking, life-changing, and it changed my outlook on expectations forever.

He said, "Simone, you want something from me that I can't provide!" *A phone call?* I wondered. To me, it seemed like such a small task, but to him, it was too much to ask. To me, it's a gift to be able to pick up the phone to speak with someone that I think about every day, but to him, it was like giving that person the world. With tears in my eyes, I got quiet, told him it's all good, and we hung up. The next time we spoke was months later.

After that phone call, many things clicked for me, but most of all, I realized the power and danger of having expectations. When I first reached out to my dad, I expected us to have an immediate bond, for him to be apologetic and for him to adjust his entire world because I was now in the picture. Instead, I got the complete opposite. At the time, it was one of the most painful emotional experiences I had ever gone through, but now that I look back, I'm so grateful that I reached out and felt the pain. It molded me.

After days of crying, missing class and being alone with my thoughts, I thought about *The Four Agreements* once again and came to the understanding that my pain was largely the result of my expectations. Having high expectations of people leads us to constantly put heavy pressure on them to do more and to be more when they don't have the same morals as we do, the capacity that's required and/or the mental strength it takes. Expectations also don't allow people to be who they truly are, and they don't allow us to accept people for who they are and for what they can provide. This is why we often end up disappointed. This is why I ended up disappointed.

So why did I set these expectations? Why did I go into the relationship with such high hopes for us? It's simple. I believed that his time was something that he *should* share with me as a father. He should care, should call, should visit and should be there, but when he wasn't, I realized that he doesn't *have to* do any of these things. They're not mandated or owed to me; I simply expected them. It was at that moment that I understood the difference between us doing things because we should do them and us doing things because we have to do them. The only things we have to do are breathe, eat, drink water and get sleep. If not, we won't survive. What we should do, on the other hand, is be great parents, friends, family members and humans. This realization is one I've carried with me ever since, and it has helped me develop a powerful sense of gratitude. Because I now know that everything people do for me or share with me is way more than they have to, I'm grateful for all they do because no one owes me anything. I'm the only one who owes me.

After gratitude, forgiveness naturally followed. Acceptance too. I forgave him for his absence and his lack of interest, and I fully accepted that he is who he is. He probably just didn't want kids, and that's okay because everyone doesn't have to be a parent.

As I look back, I feel so at peace with where we are in our relationship. We talk on birthdays (with maybe one or two calls in between), he feels no pressure to be who he isn't, and I feel no pressure to expect anything that he cannot provide. Our relationship is what it is, it's growing how it's supposed to grow, and I'm thankful for where we both are.

Note: If you currently feel the same way about a loved one, try one of these four things: (1) adjust your expectations (2) remove all expectations and accept the person for who he/she is (3) include people in your life who can meet your expectations or (4) fall back and give people the time they need to grow into who they are meant to be.

Self Love Needs Room to Breathe

Today, I am completely in love with my journey and my life in general, as I'm thankful for everyone and everything (blessings and lessons included). I've realized that both the highs and the lows are necessary parts of my life, and without them, I don't have a story to tell, a way to inspire people or the wisdom needed to keep growing in life.

Pain and confusion translate into lessons, and lessons help us breathe easier and see clearer. When I learned the greatest lesson of all—that no one owes me anything—I was able to be a more confident, peaceful and grateful person. Once I became this person, I learned to love myself without being consumed by others' lack of love toward me or their refusal to accept me. I also learned to be grateful for and to truly love those who consistently show up and do more than they have to (Mom, Grandma and Auntie, for example). When I finally loved myself and others in this new way, I was able to breathe easier and see my visions, purpose and future clearer.

Note: Give yourself permission to love you. All of you. Learn to develop a healthy relationship with yourself and to honor what you see, feel and desire. No one owes this to you.

"*Give yourself permission to love you. All of you. Learn to develop a healthy relationship with yourself and to honor what you see, feel and desire. No one owes this to you.*"

SIMONE "SAGE REEDS"

IIII

COURAGE

"History has shown us that courage can be contagious, and hope can take on a life of its own."

~MICHELLE OBAMA

10

A NAKED CONVERSATION

"We are powerful because we have survived, and that is what it is all about- survival and growth."
—Audre Lorde

MANOUCHKA " SANDIE" DOREUS

DEDICATION

To my mother who taught me that it's okay to growl at people, and to my sweet niece, NoNa, who I will continue to teach the same. To my father that taught me the strength and humility of tender love. To my sisters, Nana and Skittles, who kept it 1000 with me, your honesty kept me honest with who I was. To my Aunt Sandra, you spoke life into dead bones and I love your love. I will honor you always.

Nobody likes to talk about the quiet desperation of a wounded soul. When we think of the "depressed person" we think of averting our eyes when they look at us. We think about how sad they look, and it makes us uncomfortable. It's easy to laugh it off.

We've all been in the situation where a circle of friends is bringing up the funny way a desperate, weird energy of a person dresses strangely, or doesn't speak up, or stutters when they do. The group laughs and moves on, partly because it's all true and partly because the fact each person in the group is grateful they are "normal" enough to belong to one another. Later, you might think about this person and feel guilty because you know they need to belong. You know they need love. They need support. But it's like looking at a homeless person. We have what they need, but there is a fear that we don't have enough for ourselves, much less enough to support another human being. Everyone can think of that person in their life. They might have a kicked puppy dog look about them. Most people avoid them or they avoid people. They typically spend very little time with other people and aren't well socialized to the point of coming across rude or standoffish. In any case, they live in a bubble that is hard to penetrate even if some kind person would like to. Despite this, they need the connection desperately. Their puppy dog eyes beg for it in the moments before they break eye contact with you.

I know this because I have been that person. Sometimes I still am. People know me for my poetry. They know me for the words that I couldn't help but allow to burst from my fingertips. More recently, people have known me for the amount of energy I put into growth in all areas of life. I hope one day people know me for the amount of energy I put into loving others. Depending on how long they've known me, they've known me for my pain. I've been hurt before. I've been depressed. I have, at points in my life, been unable to make eye contact or hold long conversations. I have been written off as "not valuable".

It was in this place that I found myself at age nineteen. I was wandering. Broken. Directionless. This may come as a shock to some people, because many make assumptions about people's internal state based on their external circumstances. That's a mistake. People would congratulate me on how much I'd achieved. I hated them for not being able to really see me. What they could see with their physical eyes didn't justify my response. I was a phenomenal student for most of my life. I was, and still am, a very good poet. I enjoyed school. For the most part, I went to school, came home, went to church three times a week, and socialized very little with friends because I was goal oriented. I graduated from the International Baccalaureate Program with a 4.3 GPA. I was part of the National Honors Society. I'd been a gifted writer and impressed my teachers regularly with the depth and scope of insight on whatever subject I chose to care enough to address ...But those were few and far in between.

The truth is I cared very little for anything, and least of all, for myself. I was burning with anger and rage and apathy. Stronger than anything else was the apathy. I just didn't care. I'd reached a point in my life where trauma owned me. I was functioning on autopilot. Beneath the exterior of the model student that got good grades and perfect scores on state exams, I struggled to brush my teeth or wash my hair because it felt pointless. I was a slave to the idea that I wasn't worth the time it took. It was deeper than that. There was no conscious understanding I wasn't worth that. But it was the underlying assumption that kept me from maintaining the cleanliness of my room and even my body. This lack of self-worth translated to flunking out of one of the most prestigious HBCUs (Historical Black Colleges and Universities).

I lost a full scholarship to Howard University because rather than go to class, rather than even showering I stayed in bed and watched Netflix day after day for what amounted to the entire first semester of college. I didn't just watch TV. I watched tv, laid in bed, and ate, and I ate. I ate until I was doubled over in pain and the minute the pain subsided, I would order something else and eat again. Food had been my first comfort and now it was a drug. It sedated me. For days I would lay in the same clothes on the same bed with my laptop on my chest watching show after show of content I wouldn't even remember. I would only shower out of guilt of knowing my roommate could probably smell me. That amounted to a shower about once every two weeks.

I had no hope. At the time, I had social anxiety so bad it took me a full day to recover from meeting the other girls of the quad. I learned later through one of the very few friends I made that the encounter had left the girls feeling like I was stuck up and standoffish. It hurt me deeply that they couldn't see the situation for what it actually was. And what was it? It was bondage.

I was suffering for something that had absolutely not a damn thing to do with me. I had done nothing wrong. But somebody had. And it made me ashamed of myself. I created a dark space within me that put me in social and relational situations that were out of character with the upbringing that I had. These situations only deepened my guilt. Before I address the root, I'll show the fruit that it produced. The kind of fruit that left my mother ashamed every time she noticed it.

I would browse dating and chat sites and talk to men ten to fifteen years older than me. The conversations were never church sanctioned. I got so many phones taken away from me between the ages of thirteen and seventeen that my mom didn't even bat an eye when I got my own phone. She expected it. I was sexually active at fourteen, and when I say sexually active, I'm referring to the actual deed done in and of my own volition. I was truly active well before then, talking to boys, fulfilling little fantasies that their young and inexperienced minds thought were a big deal. I already had enough experience to think of it as child's play.

At the age of majority, the stakes changed. In DC, I found older men. Some powerful men; Politicians and lobbyists. Sex was transactional for me by that point. Love didn't factor in. I thought it was childish and naïve. Occasionally, I would build a connection, but I didn't feel worthy of pursuing any kind of relationship. The reality at that point was I didn't know how to build a relationship outside of a sexual one. It was so ingrained in my spirit to pursue a sexual relationship first that I didn't have many female friends. Most of my friends were male because I knew how to appeal to their sexual nature, whether that translated in actively having sex with them or not. I would be or say whatever they wanted, for no other reason than knowing they wanted it.

The easy route for you as the reader, is to judge the fruit. It's pretty dark. It describes a loose and promiscuous woman. "Where are her morals?" That's the easy route. But I grew up in the Christian faith. I would urge you to take the narrow path. The path that regards a sinner as a victim in their own way. And believe me when I say I have been a victim.

So here was another perspective of my childhood. I was raised in an extremely religious environment. To this day, I can recite books and chapters of the bible backwards if you wanted, despite not having read the good book in years. I was raised in a two-parent household. I had eleven aunts and uncles on my mothers' side, most of which I saw weekly, one of which I saw too often.

My memory is dodgy for most of this period, but the first encounter was one I remember explicitly. I'll spare you the details, but I was five or six years old when I woke up to find my uncle was babysitting and my parents were gone somewhere, and I thought nothing of it. When he brought me into the guestroom, despite the fact I had been warned explicitly never to go in there, I was worried, but I followed orders.

"Respect your elders," was a mantra my Caribbean family held strongly to. I had no choice but to do what I was told. When my uncle molested me with no force, but quiet commands, I followed them, despite the sirens exploding in my little five or six year-old brain. For the next five years, he came over often. At some points he was coming over weekly. He would tell me what to do, and I would do it and eventually, he expected me to anticipate what he wanted. And that is the root of it. This started the cycle of people pleasing and low self-esteem.

I hated him for it. My mom used to leave leg quarters defrosting in the sink. When I saw it, I knew my role was to cut and clean the meat for her to cook when she got home from working her twelve to sixteen hour shift. In the middle of one of those food prep situations, my uncle came to the house. This was several years into the grooming process; I know the routine. This time I decided not to follow it. He walked in, said hello to my sisters and headed towards the room. I didn't follow. He doubled back and looked at me. At this point in the process, I was cutting chicken quarters into three pieces. The knife wasn't that sharp, but it got the job done. He looked at me and I looked at the knife in my hand. I'd fantasized about redefining the lines of our relationship before. This felt like the moment that I could re-establish my right to my own body. I didn't like the secrecy. I didn't like the lies. I positioned the knife in my hand so my intent was clear.

He looked at the knife I held in my right hand, the one that was between us, and cocked his head. He asked, "Are you going to stab me?" He was mocking me. I put the knife down and follow the script.

It's from points like this that I learned self-deprecation. I couldn't even defend myself. I hated myself for lying so often. I was a child, but a child of a mother who had experienced the same trauma in her life and who asked, often, if anything like this was going on. I lied every time. Knowing what I knew about my mother's history made it a betrayal in my own eyes. I had no backbone. I was a coward. At the age of eleven, I told a friend what had happened to me. She did the only right thing in the situation. She told an adult. Within an hour of divulging information that had been so close to my chest, I was sitting in a counselor's office, unable to speak the words that she already knew. I did the only thing I could. I asked if I could write them instead. Coward.

When I took the bus home, my stomach was in knots. I imagined running away so I wouldn't have to face my mother's disappointment. I thought to myself how ironic it was that though I had fantasized often about freeing myself from this burden, I had always imagined it to be a willing and triumphant victory rather than an accident that left me like a deer in headlights. Coward.

When I got home, I could feel my mother's eyes burning into my neck. My back stayed turned to her so I wouldn't have to meet her eyes. Coward.

When I woke up the following morning, we rode up to the DCF building in silence. She asked me a single question that morning. "Is there anything you want to tell me"? I shook my head no. Coward.

And on and on the self-bashing went. Soon it wasn't just me. My mother's family couldn't imagine that their not-so-innocent younger brother could have done anything like this and so naturally I was lying. Because I'd shown signs of sexuality early on in life, I was a whore and probably pregnant and must have needed a scapegoat. Never mind that the behavior I showed was textbook behavior of a molested child. The irony was that most of my mother's family were well-educated and likely had a textbook knowledge of what the signs for my behaviors were. But when you have something to defend, and in this case, it was their adult brother over their barely prepubescent niece, what you were taught couldn't compare to what your heart knew. And what their heart knew was they loved their brother dearly.

So, lesson number one for me, I learned at eleven years old: you are not owed protection. You are not owed a tribe that will defend. It seems like a strange lesson to learn. It is not full of love and light and progress as most people with valuable life lessons would like you to believe all lessons are, but it taught me to have an honest and clear understanding about people. People are heart led. I don't expect the best of people, I expect that pressure will reveal what they care about most. The second part to this lesson, the part of it that makes it a lesson and not a deep-seated seed of **bitterness**, came much later.

That being said, at eleven years old, it was **bitterness**. I hated my family. I hated how they kept their children away from me as if I might taint them. I hated the lies and the whispers and the false smiles. I hated how nobody wanted to talk about it. I hated that I had no guidance. And I hated that I felt responsible for this new divide. Where my family had, at one point, gotten together for every gathering and met at each other's houses routinely, they now met in small groups. Some people only vibed with certain other people while others decided not to come around. Then there were those who would leave when I was around. I had a cousin that blamed me explicitly for the loss of his relationship with his uncle. He, who had lived through other allegations against another family member, felt the women in our family were manipulators who lied for gain. I don't know what they thought I would gain at the age of eleven. I just know it hurt. Worse than all of that, was that over time, being called a liar consistently made me doubt the soundness of my mind. Maybe I had made the whole thing up. Maybe I was a **liar**.

There were other factors. I was isolated. My mother, who had already been extra vigilant, could think of no other way of protecting me than to lock me away. I didn't go to anything after school. I didn't spend any time unsupervised with any person for any reason. This was more for her peace of mind than for mine. My being wounded triggered her old wounds. I was punished for not saying something sooner. I was punished for being unable to speak about it. One of her first reactions was a question, "How could you do this to me?"

I was my mother's "big-boned" child. Her family was a family of dancing women. They were beautiful chocolate goddesses with lithe figures and very active. I took after my dad's family: wide, heavy-set women with beautiful skin and hair, but I was an embarrassment to her, and she let me know it. I already felt "other" and "different" and "lesser than". Now I was a source of disappointment and pain in a way I felt I didn't have control over.

With time, my negative emotions nourished the environment for hate to build and compound and flourish so that it became the only thing that I saw. After a certain point in my life, when someone complimented me, my knee-jerk reaction was to identify them to be a liar. There was no way I could be beautiful; don't you see how much weight I've gained? I began to assign blame. I tried not to hold it against my mother. After all, I felt **guilty**. She had put so much energy into educating me against becoming a victim of abuse, and yet, here we were. I felt like I deserved for her pain to spill over me the way it did. But time passed. While she defended me like a lioness against her siblings, those same claws cut deep into me often. And I started to hate her deeply, not just for the pain she caused me, but for the pain she inflicted on my father and sisters.

My negative emotions produced an even darker fruit. My trauma would spill out in ways I felt I had no control over. I remember one day, on my way to work my night shift as a CNA at a hospital, I began keying cars in the parking garage. I scraped everything I could get into contact with. It felt good to do damage. Another day, I would stick gum to the buttons on the elevator, just to cause the next passenger some discomfort. I couldn't stand happy people. In my mind, diseased with pain, happy people had to be lying. "Hurt people hurt people," isn't a joke or a game. It's not something your rusty dusty aunt says just to get you to act right or explain away your generational curse of mommy issues.

The other less caustic but debilitating fruit of the trauma was my inability to trust people or connect. It was what had me reacting to the other girls of the quad so unsure of myself and them. It was what kept me isolating myself from people that loved me. I could never believe they actually loved me. I could never believe I was lovable. Trust was broken so early, I never learned to handle the world with any openness. I felt helplessly shut out and unworthy.

I could go on and on about the sources and expressions of my rage and pain. Some were more founded than others. But the result was that processing this pain became more important than breathing for me, but it also became terrifying. This was the reason why, at age nineteen, I would just eat, and watch shows. There was no light in life for me, because I didn't understand and was too afraid to explore the darkness I felt in myself. I avoided the pain. I numbed it. I repeated actions taught to me before I knew what they meant or would produce. Trauma and the avoidance of it created cycles in my life. I would hit highs and lows.

A low point: first winter break from college, my GPA was 1.08 and I came home after my first four months of school, 40 lbs. heavier. I wasn't allowed to sleep in my mother's house. My mother had found out I had been bringing friends (and boyfriends) into her house before going off to college. I stayed at an aunt's house instead. At night, I would stare at the ceiling and beg that God would take my life because the emotional pain was breathtaking. It literally felt like a weight on my chest. I thought God had answered that wish when I accidently broke the soap holder in the bathroom. I had braced myself against it and as it broke, it cut very near to my wrist. I cried because it didn't go all the way through. I still have the scar to prove it.

A high point: The semester after, I found a soul friend. We had gone to middle school together and had just happened to be in the same dorm, on the same floor, right as I was renewing my faith in God. She was also on a new journey to reconnect with spirit. Our cooperation towards this goal nourished me and carried me through until I could get back home to Jacksonville and my family. We prayed together. I got some of the weight off my chest. I told her how I felt out of control and how my sexuality had become a chain and a burden to me. When I "messed up" in the form of collecting a body I really didn't want, I cried on her lap, and she prayed for me when I couldn't. When I felt lost and broken, she stroked my hair, and we wrote poems together and for each other. I laughed and connected in a way that I did not think was possible for me. I still have some of those poems today and I am forever grateful to D.W. She was the first in a couple of really strong and deep bonds that kept me here.

A low point: Walking the ramp to my job, I knew the weight on my body would kill me. I remember thinking to myself that some pseudo psychologist identified rapid weight gain in trauma victims as a way to keep people and potential harm away. It was insulation. I also remember thinking my uncle was still managing to kill me. I knew he was not putting a spoon to my mouth or a gun to my head, but I blamed him for it all the same.

I gained weight trying to hide my feelings. I'd eat in secret after having a full meal with family to hide the frequency and amount I was eating. I wasn't fooling anybody and the hurt was still there after every bingeing episode. I took sexual partners that I wasn't interested in at all and pretended to enjoy the act so I wouldn't have to ever admit I didn't know how to say no. I isolated myself because I knew the self-hatred I felt was palpable and unpalatable. I didn't want to burden people with my presence.

In these low points I hit some of the worst of my self-victimization. I blamed others for all of my problems and took very little responsibility for my actions. I kept asking myself, "Why am I back to this point after feeling better?" I noticed in the moments I was intentional about taking action on my behalf to correct some mistake or fix some problem, my life improved. I also noticed that the moment my life improved, I would grow complacent and fall back into the same patterns of behavior and thought that brought me to the low emotional state I would find myself in periodically. I realized the work that I did to get to these "high points" was superficial and didn't address the root issues. After spending years with so much anger, it becomes part of you. For me, I knew the behaviors that came with my pain were unacceptable. They weren't conducive to the life I wanted to live, but rather than expose them and cut the infection out of me, I hid it and allowed it to fester. That was a costly mistake.

None of these behaviors served me. They all exposed the very pain I was trying to hide. I wasn't fooling anyone.

So, what did I do?

I got naked with myself and others.

To anyone that has experienced any sexual related trauma, you may be able to identify with the fear of exposing yourself. Not physically, but mentally and emotionally. The reason I use the phrase "get naked" is because when you undress a mind that you worked so hard to keep covered and "safe" the vulnerability is like being butt-naked in a public place with everyone in the world watching. People with an inner child to protect hate the feeling. But it must be done.

Some people are artists. They can draw their souls on paper. Other people make music that makes the world blush. ("Strumming my pain with his fingers..." Thank God for Lauren Hill). Luckily, poetry has been with me for a long time. Poetry made my self-exposure more palatable. I would write such dark, desperate little poems. I had been doing it since age eleven. It released some of the pressure. But things changed for me. I could no longer walk around with a diary and write little angry poems in secret. I needed people to see me. I needed to connect.

Soon I found myself in open mics in D.C. I would go at the request of my friend D.W. and shyly perform a couple words here and there. I would change the words at the last minute out of embarrassment of how much of myself I was exposing on stage. Eventually, I got stronger.

Eventually, that wasn't enough. I needed the people that raised me and had watched me become some darling darkling to **understand** my frustration. My poetry got deeper. I put it on social media. Sometimes it was desperately sad, other times violently angry. Sometimes the heavy sexual references in them caused friction. My mother was often embarrassed.

This was part of it. Getting naked is about exposing your truth. At the time, these were my truths. They were scary and not socially acceptable, because abuse isn't socially acceptable. It isn't polite or inviting. It isn't warm. It is and will always be uncomfortable and people will be unforgiving for making them uncomfortable too. I'm sure some of my family, both immediate and extended, will feel that by writing even this, I am attacking them. But it is my truth, and I won't apologize for it.

Neither should you. The mantra for my generation is, "Express yourself."

Although I agree that a lot of my generation takes this as license to offend at will, it's important. Not being able to speak is considered a disability. Being mute will get you government dollars whether it interferes with your functioning or not. Life is about inhale and exhale, and when you don't do either of those things you die. When you experience pain and don't release it; when you eat and don't release it; when you drink too much water even; you die.

I learned the necessity of **honesty**. And if I'm being honest, I learned it too well. I was rude at that time. I was cold. When people spoke to me, I wouldn't respond because I just honestly didn't want to. I now understood I didn't have to lie. I don't think I could've lied if I wanted to. This was the longest most disrespectful exhale of my life.

A lot came out of it. My mother and I had hard conversations about our relationship. Thoughts that I had kept to myself previously, due to the Caribbean upbringing of respecting your elders, turned into ugly confrontations. We addressed a lot in that time. We healed a lot in that time and the things that couldn't be addressed to my satisfaction, I released. I also identified people that could listen to me exhale and supported me through it. Some people became a diary for me. By no means am I saying to vomit your pain over any and everybody, but if you remember lesson one, then know there is a flipside.

The other side of the coin of lesson one: You are not owed a tribe, but **there are people that will fight for your soul.** And it may not be the person that you thought would do it. For me it was my aunt Sandra and my baby sister. My aunt actively pulled me out of some of the darkest places of my life. My sister would just lay the entire length of her body over mine, and it soothed me. I couldn't let anyone touch me, but she could, just off of the strength of who she was. Be grateful for these people and cherish them.

It taught me the second part of my healing, which is, **to understand what you're healing from and what you are progressing to**. For the first time in my life, I set goals and expectations for my relationship with people and with men. I wrote about love at this point. I finally admitted that I deeply valued family and wanted that for myself, though I'd had a deep-seated fear of pregnancy and no faith in marriage. This was due, in part, to the fact that my family had expected pregnancy from me from the moment they knew what happened to me and I had to prove them wrong, but also because I was convinced I would ruin my children with my inner turmoil. At this point in life, my poetry was about insomnia and the life I wanted but didn't feel worthy of having. "Know thyself" was my mantra. I had to understand who I was. I had to separate what was the trauma, and what was my own desire. Sometimes it was harder than others. I experienced several relationships that taught me about myself and my boundaries. I learned I could love. I learned not everyone deserved it.

I healed to a degree. I felt better. The 1.18 GPA that I left Howard with, was now a solid 3.0. I had focused on a major in my junior year of college. Psychology. I was determined to heal myself completely. I could focus on a goal and see it through. I was learning to regulate my eating habits. I began watching motivation videos and reading books on growth. I had taken up affirmations, the first set of which had brought a flood of tears over me because it was hard to believe I was beautiful and healthy and whole and defended. It got easier with time. I no longer wanted to die.

Most importantly, my newfound honesty sparked a conversation. I didn't mean it to. I won't pretend to take credit for the outcome. My family had built a group chat. Over a decade has gone by since news of my abuse hit the air. Like with all families, there has been a ton of other little happenings and falling outs and falling back ins. I woke one morning to my family congratulating each other on how far they had come. The truth is that they had grown through a lot together, as do all families. But there was a seed of a lie there. The hypocrisy was too much for me. I asked one question. I don't know what my purpose was. Maybe the purpose was just to cause confusion. It was just my truth. The question was: If we are so whole and healed, where is uncle ------?

While I can't answer the question of what my purpose was, I can tell where the question came from. As I said earlier, the family hardly came together as a unit. Either I was somewhere, or he was. If I was somewhere, I never saw certain people. If he was there, it was the same. So, while a family that had condemned me at eleven were celebrating the health of the family, I wanted the whole truth exposed.

What came of the question wasn't what I was expecting. Of course, the question was ignored by most of the family. I don't mean that to sound petulant. But someone took notice. That someone was my uncle's wife, who had been in the group chat. She told him. He reached out to me. I was terrified. In my mind, the only reason an abuser would reach out to the victim of their abuse after said victim called them out, was to bully them into silence. He asked to meet up. I agreed. I wasn't going to hide, and I wasn't going to lie. I felt I had done both of those things for too long.

I will never forget sitting in that booth. I won't forget the dinner. I remember sitting in Johnny Rockets, and ordering cake because my nerves were frazzled, and sugar was my drug of choice. It was vanilla bean cake and too sweet. I couldn't swallow it. I arrived early, because my anxiety dictated that I always arrived early, and I sweat like a silverback gorilla. I prayed and I cried, and I wiped tears because he didn't deserve to see them. And I could barely breathe.

When he showed up, he was right on time, I wished I had picked a spot at the bar. I still wasn't sure what he wanted to say to me, but I wanted to be angry. I wanted him to give me the opportunity to lash out. He didn't.

He apologized.

At that moment, I knew two things. The first was that I wanted my freedom. Up until this moment I had been begging for freedom. I was begging to whatever God would listen. If the devil could do it, I would allow him. I didn't care. That depressed period of my life had seemed never ending. So, the second thing I absolutely knew in my heart, was if I truly wanted to be free- if I wanted it to be like this trauma and pain had never happened- I had to forgive him and never pick up that burden again. I didn't know what that looked like exactly, but the prosperity and beauty I needed in my life depended on it.

I felt I deserved it after a youth spent in what felt like hell. So, I told him I forgave him and retreated to work out what that actually meant.

What that actually meant was months of conversation where he talked about where he was in life and how he got there. We spoke about his children. About a spiritual awakening he felt he was having. About his reaction to my forgiveness, but not about my trauma. Not about my pain. I was afraid to bring it up. I felt it would violate the understanding I had with myself. - I had to forgive him and never pick up that burden again.

In those months, I chose instead to see him as a human being. Amazing things happened in that time. My healing deepened. My father had been deeply wounded when he found out what had happened to me. I met my uncle at the same diner one day for him to tell me he had driven to my parents' house at five am to beg my father's forgiveness. Me choosing to forgive this man had opened the door for my sweet and humble father to get back some kind of recompense for his own pain. Obviously, it wouldn't reverse what happened, but this was more than I thought I would ever get. I held onto the idea of seeking freedom rather than chasing pain.

My uncle had accidentally convinced me to go vegan. Accidentally, because he only meant to imply that eating healthier was a choice, but my understanding at the time was that veganism was the healthiest choice. I felt so empowered by my decision to face him, and impressed that good things had come of it, that I took it all the way and lost over fifty lbs. in a matter of two to three months. I just knew that as long as I sought freedom over revenge and let that pain go, I would be free.

But I allowed myself to be knocked off my square. My uncle had gotten progressively more adamant that he was having a spiritual experience. I believed him. We reached a point where we hadn't spoken for at least two months. I was over the contact. I had gotten what I needed. But he and his "spiritual experience" reached a fever pitch. It was manic and insane and while I had a textbook knowledge of it, it was still frightening and triggered me.

On this particular day, I want to say I was especially tired. I don't know if it was true, but I got a call from my uncle late in the day. He called me and, for the first time, made excuses for what he had done to me. He claimed he was the result of a sexual tryst between his mother and one of his half-brothers. He said my mother had confided something in him and told me what it was. He told me every secret about every person he knew and an assortment of other things which he concluded by stating that these were the reasons he was messed up enough to do what he did to me.

I tried to handle it maturely. I got off the phone and tried to meditate. I tried to pray. I tried to breathe, but my breath was ragged and shallow, and I was so angry. How dare he justify his sins with what others had done, and how dare he further disrupt my relationship with family that was already so delicate and that I had tried so hard to restore and repair? How dare he pour his trauma and pain into me. Had he not already caused me enough pain?

For the first time in a while, the focus was no longer on me and what I could do to improve my experience. It was now about what he had done to me. It was a moment I wasn't prepared for. I couldn't understand how he could possibly justify the pain he caused. So, I lit into him in the only way I knew how. I wrote out in detail every pain and every consequence of his actions. I started with my sexual habits and dysfunctions and ended with the barrier he had helped build between me and my mother. I added the depression, how I had sabotaged every relationship, and how I committed to relationships that were terrible for me. I listed thinly veiled prostitution and my inability to connect and ended with how we would never have a normal natural relationship because he had violated me and so I had been avoiding him for months.

It was exhilarating. It was the moment I had wanted in the diner. It felt so good. It felt Godly even. But it was wrong. It violated the freedom I asked for because me and God had an understanding. My job was to let it go so God could negotiate and broker my freedom. The results of my action were two-fold. The following morning, he apologized again and stated he was going to church. He seemed calm and collected and I didn't think anything of it. Around six pm I received a call from my Aunt Sandra. She told me my uncle was in jail and asked if I had anything to do with it. The whole world stood still for me. I had nothing to do with it, but part of me felt vindicated. I still do. He had turned himself in.

Even though the police had been involved the first time around, they couldn't prove anything as I had given "conflicting statements" as a child; they couldn't charge him.

Now he had walked himself into the station and told them everything. Not only that, but the same way I had felt crazy before, he was apparently manifesting now. They were considering it a psychotic break. It felt too good to be true. It felt like God himself was balancing a scale that had been thrown out of kilter when I was an eleven year-old girl. I had no real interest in him being punished. It didn't help my healing process at all. It wouldn't heal my wounds. But the idea that the bondage I felt, he would now feel, felt good. I felt I deserved this moment.

What I didn't feel I deserved, came after. Those messages I had so wisely captured forever via text messages that outlined my pain? His wife found them and distributed them to the family. It was on the family group chat. The irony was sadistically beautiful. My mother was deeply hurt by my response to what he'd said about her. The family now had detailed information on how far I had gone. I had always done my best to protect myself from their judgmental disposition towards me. But in this case, I had exposed myself. By lashing out at him, I had made myself a victim again. I exposed myself. Against my own judgment and against the understanding I had with myself, I had created an environment to victimize myself again. This lapse in judgement is fine by some people's estimation. It was right and just by the way others evaluated it. But based on the standard I set for myself it was wrong and caused me pain. This wasn't up for debate.

I started spiraling again. I gained back the fifty lbs. over time. I wasn't as bad as I had been before. I had learned things the first time around; I loved exercise for one. I now enjoyed spending some time with some people. But I wasn't functioning at my highest level and my victim mentality lurked in my mind. I wanted to blame him. I wanted to blame his wife. But I remembered who I was and who I wasn't, and I rebuilt.

The journey back wasn't necessarily important. What was important was the mindset that got me here. I have decided, then and now, to never again be a victim. I am a survivor, always. If you are a victim, I would suggest you redefine the lines and make yourself a survivor. Survivors don't suffer for the sake of suffering. They grow from suffering.

What Does This Mean for YOU?

If you are asking yourself the question I asked myself for years; if you can't make heads or tails of your situation and you need to know the how of it; if you just know you will do anything to get free and just need a direction to head towards, I can help you. I want to help you. I have to help you.

The question: How do I make this pain end?

The answer isn't something I can give you. It's not short; it takes time. It's not chronological; you will find yourself stuck in loops and cycles. You can and will make it out. Here are some places to start.

1. Stop rehearsing and replaying your trauma and pain. You cannot be a victim if you are to be an overcomer. Choose to no longer be a victim.

Replaying your trauma over and over strengthens its hold over you. It reinforces the negativity in your life. I nursed the wound for years. It doesn't help. In fact, it causes more harm.

That being said, you have to study your own life. Look for cause and effect. He hurt me and so my response was xyz. Xyz led to 123. 123 caused a triangle squared and I'm still messed up about it. I've got to stop doing xyz. Why am I doing xyz? What are my triggers?

Focus on the emotions causing the actions. The core emotions for me are betrayal, hate, pain, and guilt. The specific emotions don't matter. They may not be the same for you, but in a lot of cases they will be. What matters is what you felt. You must identify the root to kill the tree.

 * Notice I say isolate the core emotions rather than focus on what was done to you.

2. Empower yourself to move and do for yourself and agree with yourself to do whatever that needs to be done.

 This doesn't include killing your abuser or harming yourself. I wouldn't have included this if it wasn't a thought that visited me often. This does include purging. This includes getting honest and buck for yourself. This includes sitting in a psychologist's office, walking out on them in the middle of their sentence and coming back a few weeks later. This includes leaving class abruptly to go sing to yourself in the stairwell to calm your spirit. At least that is what it looked like for me. You will offend people. You will offend people that don't deserve it. It's okay. They will live.

3. Humble yourself so that you can make amends.

Sometimes it's not just them. Sometimes it's you. Your trauma will and has manifested in ugly ways. Trauma is the gift that keeps giving. Rather, it is the shit that flows downhill. You may have wounded other people. You will offend people that don't deserve it. But you aren't an island. You need and deserve connection and relationship and love. If that means humbling yourself and apologizing for calling your mother a whore in a series of text messages she was never supposed to see (even if part of you felt some type of way), buckle up buttercup, because that is what you are going to do. You don't have the right to deny yourself love and support. You of all people need it most.

4. DO NOT pick your pain up after you release it.

This step is a BS step. The truth is you will keep picking it up until you learn and become strong enough to leave it down. But FOR THE LOVE OF GOD, do your very best to leave it down.

I retraumatized myself at twenty three after I thought the pain was gone for good. My family reading those text messages brought back the pain and fear and exposure that I felt at age eleven when the first set of rumors circulated. Little did people know, the deeper trauma for me was how I lost faith in family and people. That was the trauma I'm still working through today. That was the trauma I have to fight to put down. It makes social situations awkward for me and I remind myself to breathe through them every so often. But that is another book for another day.

5: **Stop trying to be NORMAL. There is no such thing.**

The truth about trauma and freedom from it, is the same truth that drug addicts learn on day one: It happened, whatever it is and now you must daily decide to be free. It will get easier with practice. It is a muscle. You can get to a point where you function "like it never happened". But it did happen. And when you heal from it colors will be brighter, every relationship that is good and healthy in your life will be that much more beautiful, and you will be grateful for everything. You will see colors other people have no words for.

You will also hurt differently and at different triggers than others. Learn to manage it. Things that other people hurt about, you will not care about. Learn to be sympathetic. It doesn't make you a monster that you don't care what happened in that explosion in Paris because you are dealing with your own real-world holocaust.

"...It's been weeks
Since I didn't have to force a smile
But everything anyone wants to talk about
Is the damn awards shows
That seem to be happening every week now
And I'm weak now
But all I seem to be able to do is speak now
Full of words but every sound that comes out
Brands me as a mute

And a liar on the rebound..."

age 19

That poem basically sums it up. There is more to the poem, but focus on this: I was trying hard to appear healthy here; pretending I cared about things I clearly didn't. And people could tell I was forcing it. I could tell and I was losing respect for myself for pretending. If you don't care, be honest about who you are and where you are right now. You don't have to care. Your job is not to fit in. You don't have to give a flip about the Olympics or the BET awards. You have to get healthy and whole first. You don't even have to care after getting healthy and whole.

6. **Focus on you.**
This really needs no explanation, but it's so important. It takes work. It takes journaling. It's about real conversations with yourself and choosing you AT ALL COST. Not your raggedy boyfriend that makes you feel good temporarily. Not your mother with health issues from living an unhealthy life. If you are unhealthy, you aren't in any position to help anyone.

I travel often now. When they give you the in-flight instructions about safety, they say always put your mask on first before trying to help anyone around you. Put it on, and make sure oxygen is flowing, then put on your child's mask. Why? Because surviving is their best chance at survival.

And what does survival look like?

I graduated with a bachelor's in psychology for no other reason than I needed to heal myself. I had to understand. I would have flunked out of school any other way and I mean that.

I'm recently engaged to a wonderful man who knows about my trauma and my trauma induced body count and he loves me like I've never been touched. We are excited to start a family and build together and travel everywhere. He proposed right after we got back from Mexico.

I just left a very good paying job in health and life insurance to follow my passion of writing with the full support of the friends and family that I keep close. I own a car rental business and recently started a real estate investment company with my sisters.

There is life after trauma. It can be real and vibrant and flowing and full of love and laughter. You can be healthy, wealthy and wise. I chose to want my freedom more than I wanted revenge or to nurse my wounds. I chose not to suppress. Yes, some old pain that needs to be addressed or readdressed comes up every so often, but I do my best to remain open to the journey.

If you are reading this because you have your own journey to start or are on it, please, please, please know that as long as there is breath in your body, there will always be hope. You aren't the first to hurt the way you do, and you will not be the last. You aren't unique in your suffering and there are people who you can relate to. You are never alone. I hope you find the peace you are looking for and that you pursue your truth.

I am so loved and protected and befriended and defended.
YOU are so loved and protected and befriended and defended.
I end every poem I post anywhere the same way. I 've been doing it for years. I'll do the same here.

#truthseeker #findingmypeace #aitheonlypoet

"...as long as there
is breath in your
body, there will
always be hope. You
aren't the first to
hurt the way you do,
and you will not be
the last. You aren't
unique in your
suffering and there
are people who you
can relate to. You
are never alone."

MANOUCHKA " SANDIE" DOREUS

11

LESSONS IN LOVE

"Love didn't hurt you. Love gave you the strength to move on, to let go, to forgive and find Love within yourself. Love saved you."
— Londrelle

LARRY "LOVE" WAKEFIELD JR.

DEDICATION

I dedicate this to my son, Seth. Also to every person who struggles with self-love. Son, may you never know what it's like to not love yourself. May boundaries with yourself and with others always exist. My people in the struggle, learn to love yourselves fully. From self-love flows the rivers of life. Get free. Stay free.

The Awakening

"Ever made love to the woman of your dreams in a room full of money out in London and she screams?"
"-Rick Ross

For some reason at sixteen years old I imagined losing my virginity to be the experience of that in these Rick Ross lyrics. I was sadly mistaken. Remember watching certain movies growing up with virginity scenes in them? Though there were those movies like *"The Wood"* or *"Love and Basketball"* where you viewed a more realistic experience of what a first time could be like, there were also more adult movies like *"Titanic"* or *"Soul Food"*. The first two movies showed actual teenagers and their first time being uncomfortable and even painful. Though *"Titanic"* and *"Soul Food"* didn't have virginity scenes, the sexual scenes, which I did see as a adolescent, were how I viewed and desired sex for myself to be.

In my young, helpless romantic mind, I just knew I was different and would experience the latter. Lots of eye gazing, slow moving, passionate kissing and the space to take my time and make love. I was in for a rude awakening as I was met with a few minutes of pleasure, a quick moment's peak and confusion on what to do next with myself next. This choice brought me to my first moment of true experience with romantic love.

I had recently broken up with my girlfriend for many, what felt like, young and dumb reasons. Looking back with my developed retrospective mind, I was honestly afraid the passion we had for one another would bloom too richly and that we might possibly be in over our heads. Especially at sixteen. Again, I'd been a hopeless romantic since adolescence. After all our passion came to an end with us breaking up I then proceeded to lose my virginity to a young lady whom I didn't have nearly as deep a connection with. I had no real reason for choosing her other than that we were sexually attracted to each other and an opportunity was presenting itself. Shortly after losing my virginity, the same day, I ended up in the same place as my ex. In normal teenage fashion one of my friends slipped up while joking and mentioned what had happened only hours before. The news was now out for the jury to know. Needless to say I broke my ex's heart that day.

Though young, based on my understanding at the time I loved her. She was genuinely a good friend of mine as well as my "girlfriend". I spent the next few hours apologizing to her and explaining why we had just broken up yet shortly after I had my "life changing" with another young woman. Was I not faithful? Has this been the plan all along? Did I not really like her? All the questions my ex asked me over and over that night. This moment transformed me forever as it started me on my true path and purpose to understanding and spreading love. Breaking the heart of someone I claimed I loved and not having sufficient answers brought me to a spiritual awakening that helped shape me into the man I am becoming today.

Growing up with a Baptist Christian upbringing; holy water, white "sacred" bibles, Italian Jesus on the wall and Sunday school in the church basement were a normal part of my every week routine. My parents were married until I was seven years old. We would wake up early Sunday mornings, get dressed and go to church with my grandmother and all my cousins on my mom's side. This wasn't every Sunday but definitely most holiday's and other random times such as baptism services or church plays.

As I grew a little older my family dynamic changed as my parents divorced and different households meant different churches. My mother and I lived with my grandmother where I was then expected to go to bible study every Sunday. This remained until my great grandmother figured we were big enough to decide on our own, which was about middle school age; twelve or so. Eventually my mom and I moved into our own place on the other side of town and I went through many different denominations after this. Each one had different ways of operating. Yet if I'm honest, I was still your typical young black boy sleeping through many services and getting up because I was told I needed to be there or else. It wasn't until about fourteen years old when true introspection happened. I started to think about career and family, what my existence meant and why I was here. My thirst for reading and real knowledge began and words I would hear over the pulpit started to connect with me spiritually.

While visiting a church with my Father and my Stepmother at the time, something the Reverend said resonated with me. He spoke of God's love for us and how much we were cherished as creation. That moment hit me differently. I asked after that week if we could come back. Shortly after that visit we joined the church as a family and I (along with my stepsiblings) were on our way to a Vacation Bible School retreat in Panama Beach, Florida. That weekend was the first time I was introduced to men who were really about their business in that church. They cared about us understanding the scriptures and how it related to our personal lives. They were open and vulnerable with us. They allowed us to share parts of ourselves that we normally didn't talk about as young black kids. Though that summer changed me from church, just being a place I needed to go to and being a place I can actually learn and apply values to my life, the school year brought me back into my normal "loving" yet teenage self.

Going to service with my mother during that school year was different. I went to youth service during the week and those words resonated differently with my young, hormone enraged self. I had urges I often didn't know how to navigate or what to do with. Looking back I'm extremely grateful for sports.

"STOP HAVING SEX! GOD IS NOT PLEASED. REPENT, FOR THE KINGDOM OF HEAVEN IS AT HAND!" My youth pastor belted out these words, which felt like ten times a sermon. Sound familiar?

Before I lost my virginity, there were constant struggles of understanding why I felt so much guilt and shame when the youth pastor would "obliterate us" with the scriptures. The conviction was real. We had been told sexual intercourse was holy and for the marriage bed only. Though I wasn't having intercourse, I was but a few steps away. My youth pastor had to know what was inside me. He just had to know what I had been contemplating. What I'd come to find out though… that "spirit" was in all of us. Of course he knew because it was inside of him! Young teenage boys (teenagers period) are struggling to find their identity. Not just in sexuality but in every facet of life. Who am I? What am I doing here? Who is God? What is love? So many questions and (at the time) seemingly not many answers. Yet one thing seemed very clear… "REPENT, FOR THE KINGDOM OF HEAVEN IS AT HAND!" Yes yet what do I do with these urges?

Here I am. Sixteen years old, having sinned before God with a girl I wasn't in love with. My ex now knew the truth and just couldn't understand how someone could say they loved you, yet hurt you this bad. She wanted me to be her first. To share that moment with someone she loved.

Lost. Confused. I knew I'd messed everything in life up. I'd ruined a great friendship and was feeling embarrassed. How could I say I loved her yet I hurt her this way? Donell Jones' song, "Where I Wanna Be" played in my head a million times as I wished I had just done what he had written about. He decided to break up with girlfriend because of all the lust that resided in him and being around so many beautiful women, he didn't want to be unfaithful. Yet truth be told, I had done that. Being a relatively new high schooler, I knew the pressures I was facing relationally and had called things off and tried to remain friends. Yet and still I ended up here. Would love really move this way? How could I say I love you and act this way? One night, a few months later, I laid in my bed experiencing what felt like mental torment. Thinking about all the women I had lusted over, girls I kissed or got extremely close to sex with. I even thought about how many of those girls I may have hurt unintentionally by moving from my urges and not love. I lamented out to God and begged, "If you take this away from me, I promise to love people fully and live my life for you." Then came my first awakening.

I felt like Paul in the bible. I was blinded by a light on this road and suddenly life became about pleasing God when before they were only about myself. I had a thirst for theology and studying the bible. All I wanted to do was understand the scriptures and know God. I knew my mind and spirit had made a shift. I was known for carrying my bible around my high school but it was also known that if you needed an ear or a hand, I was there to give it. I lost some close friends during that time and gained some new ones.

For the next two years I spent my life dedicated to the church I was in and to the God I served. Everything done was to God's glory. I led bible studies, prayed with friends and brought people with me to church. I vowed to love people the best I could and give them the truth I now knew. I graduated top of my senior class, dedicated and motivated by love to take on the world. Little did I know my lessons in love had barely begun. Right before I graduated high school, I met a woman...

Lessons In Love

Lesson number one, who you choose to love can and will impact the entirety of your life for generations to come. So choose wisely.

Right before graduating high school I met a young woman at my church who captivated me. Though only two years older, she believed I was too young for her so dating was out of the question. We became really good friends for a time and then our friendship became more. The passion between us started to rise, which was a problem because we were both devoted to God. Before we could get that handled, tragedy struck. I lost a huge Father figure in my life; my Grandfather. The loss seemed unbearable yet there she was. Though not technically my girlfriend, she stood by my side like I had only seen my family do. I instantly knew I wanted to experience that for the rest of my life with her. Marriage was huge to me growing up; as I hadn't seen many good ones yet desired to have a good one of my own. And based on where we were in our relationship, spiritually it was better to marry than to burn.

At the tender age of nineteen, I chose to marry this woman for reasons of love and obedience to God's word. We both were full time college students at the time. With only a few dollars, some dreams and tons of ambition, I was determined to make my first adult relationship last the test of time. My parents' divorce left me with a chip on my shoulder. So I vowed to love wholeheartedly and communicate in order for my marriage to succeed. There were constant conversations I had with my parents about doing better than they did. Yet there was one huge detail I failed to understand and experience had to teach me. Who you marry matters.

I grew up in a very loving yet dysfunctional family. Not many marriages lasted with the exception of my grandparents. Around me families formed, the relationship got hard, communication broke down then divorce and the breaking up of a home happened. This was the constant cycle. My then wife, on the other hand, grew up differently. Her family was from the Caribbean. Though divorce was still within her family, it wasn't the norm. No matter how much they fought and couldn't stand each other, they stayed together; even if it was to their detriment. After my parents divorce, in my household I was raised to talk if there was an issue. Even if we couldn't come to an agreement, there was a back and forth to work towards some understanding. In her household, the back and forth was hardly for understanding but more to be heard; even if it meant hurting the other person's feelings. Where I was born into a breakdown of communication that then turned to communicating for understanding, she grew up her whole life with yelling and screaming to no avail yet they won't leave because they love each other. These patterns were a part of who we were. And surely enough they caused us issues.

All of us have trauma that stems from simple yet complex issues such as effectively communicating that we are healing from in our lives. Therefore we must take the time to find out who we are truly allowing in our space of love. Ultimately, everyone has baggage from their upbringing. So when it comes to the matters of the heart and romance, who you choose to love can literally make or break you.

My next three years of our marriage were spent in a whirlwind of turmoil and heartache as we learned the truth about each other. Not only were we not compatible, our family traumas were so deep we had started to ruin one another and ourselves. We couldn't stop arguing. A disagreement would ensue and where I wanted to talk about it, she would shut down and at times even ignore me. I felt like I was married to a brick wall. Communication became non-existent on her end. In response I became very naggy as I needed communication, yet I didn't know how to communicate with her effectively especially with her not speaking. She became distant and I felt more and more like I couldn't trust her. Around and around we went.

The once sweet couple who had vowed "til death do we part" was now halfway across the country due to me joining the U.S. Air Force, in a city with all new friends and nothing to look at but one another; whom we now couldn't stand. We could feel the end coming soon. As a man, I felt crushed. As a husband, I felt like a failure. I'd joined the military in hopes to provide a more stable life for my family. We had trust and communication issues before the military yet I figured distance and a change of scenery could do us both some good. But it's true what they say, running away from your problems is a race you will never win.

Lesson number two: You can take a horse to the water but you cannot make them drink.

The end was near for our union. Everyday was simply going through the motions. Responsibilities, home, food, bed, wake up, repeat. Though we laid next to each other every night, we couldn't have been more distant. After work one day we got into a huge argument and it ended with her threatening to go back to Florida and file for divorce. We had made promises to never even use the word "divorce" and now she was threatening to file for one. I was hurt and angry yet tired and ready to give her what she was asking for. She wasn't happy and neither was I.

Then some of the most shocking news we could fathom came. We found out we were pregnant. Great! What do we do? So many questions came to mind. *Was the child mine? Was I ready? Did I really want to bring a child into the world with where we were in our relationship?* We had always wanted a family yet here we were, about to bring things to an end and now the family wanted to grow. I was still serving in the military and we were due for another move that at this point we weren't ready for.

We eventually made the move to our next duty station in the states and chose to try and stick it out for our unborn child. We found a church to attend, started counseling and doing more things together. The sun started to feel like it was beginning to shine on us. Yet I was in for one of the biggest lessons of my life. The only thing we can control as humans is ourselves.

Ever been in a conversation where someone is telling you a host of problems and to each issue you have all of the solutions? So you are waiting for them to finish spilling it all so you can drop this new revelation on their life that will change everything. Only for them to hear your advice, agree and then never take it? Now imagine that person is the closest person to you. Then imagine the advice you are giving is for your relationship to grow and be better. Yes, the pain and struggle is of the realist extent when it's in your own backyard. It affects every facet of your life. Yet what are you to do?

What I learned during that trying time was to one, realize I cannot control every outcome; especially those where other people's emotions, experience and understanding is involved. Two, we all have the power of choice. When you realize you have given all you can but you and that significant other just aren't seeing eye to eye, you can choose to agree to disagree or you can do as some people say, move around it. Avoiding it never solves anything. So ultimately you must make a decision in moving things forward. Third, we must understand that ultimately loving someone means allowing them to be as they are and while encouraging them to be their best selves, never forcing their hand. People will be who they will be. Real love guides, encourages and supports someone's growth and betterment while understanding we can make no one do.

Lesson number three: Love your neighbor as you love yourself because self-love is the best love.

This lesson has been the hardest to learn and the one I spend most of my current days living out. Despite the heartache, pain, military moves and now the pregnancy in the picture, I had come to a place of truly feeling lost. What was I doing? Why was I doing it? I didn't understand what my why was anymore. Everyday I had to search and find a reason for even getting up to go to work because I didn't have one. Depression set in and life started to have its way with me. I would only go to work and come home. When I was home I would sit on the floor in the guest room and stare at the wall for hours just thinking. I didn't find interest in the gym, music or much of anything I normally cared about. Unclear direction, constant arguments and bad decisions with money, food and my time. I had gotten to a place of desperation and darkness I had never seen before. My pregnant wife was consumed with her demons and unstable hormones and though we were living together, we were barely a step above roommates. Multiple times out of anger she would take the car and not say where she was going. One time in particular she took the one car we actually had and drove from Colorado all the way to Florida, pregnant. There was nothing I could do to stop her from acting out how she was. I was home alone, on a military base hundreds of miles away from my family. I had hit rock bottom and truly for the first time in my life contemplated not existing on this earth anymore. That moment made me realize enough was enough. This began a five year lesson for me.

In the Holy Bible, Yeshua summed up the whole ten commandments into two; to love God with our whole hearts and for us to love our neighbors as we love ourselves. That verse, even as a young teenager, stuck out to me and begged the question how much we should love ourselves? When you understand sentence structure, as we love ourselves though at the end, it is really a predicate ultimately expressing we cannot love others if we don't love ourselves. Though I didn't understand the depths of this statement at the time, I knew something was changing in my core and I needed to obey it or there would be no clear path for me as a man or a Father let alone a human being.

My wife eventually came back to where we were in Colorado and after a few frustrating counseling sessions and some odd behavior, I put two and two together and realized she wasn't being faithful to our union. She didn't notice I had found out and I hadn't planned on telling her until I was sure and I knew what was the best way to move forward. Though divorce was something I swore I'd never do, it was time to stop existing in such a negative space.

We had tried so many different ways to work through our issues together for years at this point. I felt if we couldn't figure out how to heal and work it out even with the help of God, separation and professionals, it was time to let each other go for the sake of our own sanity. She eventually flew back to Florida so we could give birth to our son there and have family support. We then had an honest conversation in which she confessed she hadn't been faithful. She mentioned how she felt alone and just wanted company which was confusing to me because we spent everyday together with the exception of our time being separated when she chose to leave. Though I understood because there were parts of me that had mentally checked out, I was at a loss for words as these feelings of loneliness were never brought to me to try and fix. I couldn't stand it any longer. I filed for divorce shortly after our son's birth.

Many couldn't understand why I had "left my family". They didn't know what was going on in our home so all they could see was a black man leaving his wife and his child, creating another broken home. Though I felt like a failure for repeating the cycle, how could I express to these people what it felt like to lose myself inside my marriage? To feel as though I was suffocating under the weight of having a healthy marriage and I didn't even know what one truly looked like. I started to realize I didn't even know who I was outside of being a married man and now a Father. What did I like to do? What made me happy? Did I even love myself? Unfortunately, I didn't.

I spent the next few years in court fighting custody battles, paying legal fees and being in and out of court. Though oftentimes it seemed she didn't want to be married while in the union, she made it very hard to leave. It became extremely draining and multiple times my parental rights were threatened to be taken away. Why did I keep going through with it?

The old saying crossed my mind often, "It's cheaper to keep her." Yet the reality was, the moment I realized I didn't want to live anymore I had tapped into a space I never knew existed.

I began to understand the true meaning of lesson three. *Out of an overflow and understanding of self-love, we are able to truly love our neighbor.*

I didn't know boundaries or what it meant to take care of myself. My family history was all about putting others' needs before yourself. We then call that love and once all love tanks are empty blaming others for draining you, ending that relationship with a bitter attitude as we watch the cycle continue. I was done with that way of living. It was time to learn from the mistakes in the living passed down to me as well as my own uninformed ways of living.

Developing A Deeper Love For Self

Choosing to love myself was one of the greatest choices I've ever made. Through persistence and honesty I was able to gain clear time with my son, my divorce came to an end which surprisingly put my now ex-wife and I in a better space to learn to co-parent. I was able to change where I served in the Air Force and my healing process began. Those questions of "what did I like to do?" and "who was I?" started to yield answers. I began to dig into fashion and fitness. I began traveling the world and experiencing new people and their cultures. New hobbies and even some forgotten passions began to resurface such as making music, writing and DJing.

I started to challenge how I ate to hit certain goals I wanted in my body. New life started to form within me. Happiness was being restored. Yet old habits die hard and life is full of lessons to be learned. As these days, weeks and months went by, I never stopped dating. Some relationships seemed promising while others were stopped abruptly as I couldn't get past a few interactions with certain women. My boundaries began to show and my discernment for people's energy became clearer. It became easier to be honest with myself with what I desired and what I wouldn't settle for. Yet in typical Larry Love fashion, I met a woman.

My life is different now. Where I once was pursuing a lifelong relationship as a nine to five military man, I was now a part-time Air National Guardsman who occasionally had to leave for duty and a full-time dad and DJ/Event Curator, which often meant late nights and early mornings. While attempting to date, many women didn't understand that. Though they may have loved watching me move around spaces how I did, it takes a different type of understanding and grace to be in continual relationship with my lifestyle. I felt I had found the one. We met within the event space. She often encouraged me to be who I was and she was extremely supportive of my DJ world and more importantly my son; as she had her own son. She was beautiful, smart, kind, spiritual, open, honest and she understood me. What more could I ask for?

One day we went to a kickback together to get out of the house. We only knew a few people there but were looking forward to meeting new people. While there I realized the woman who put the kickback together I had met before. Towards the end of the event she personally thanked everyone for coming and as she came by I reminded her of where we met. As we shared a laugh of a remembered moment I pulled my phone out and we exchanged social media accounts. This was normal practice for me as a DJ so people can keep up with what I currently have going on and reach me all in one place. I thought nothing of it. Yet when my girlfriend came to get the keys from me to sit in the car, her energy felt like an upset gust of wind and I knew I'd done something wrong. On our ride home she assured me nothing was wrong and that she was fine, yet being raised around women I just knew that wasn't the case. Sure enough, after we got the kids to bed I received the truth about what she felt. I had to have exchanged numbers in order to pursue something with the woman from the event or else why did I give her my phone? I allowed her to express what she felt and why.

I then shared what happened from my point of view yet I was sure she wouldn't believe me. After hours of back and forth, there was no avail. Changing her mind was out of the question it seemed. I was at a loss for words. We spent the next few days going back and forth which I hated doing. My go to response in times like this is to retreat. Having been to counseling I understand that is what they call shutting down and it isn't recommended in attempting to work through problems. She eventually asked for her key back and I took that as a sign that we were over. I gladly gave her back the key and went about my business. That only made the situation worse.

Why was I here again? Had I not learned my lesson? Why was love always tripping me up? The truth is, lessons never stopped having to be put into practice. And though in one space of our lives we may have conquered something, as we grow and evolve old patterns will resurface for us to continue to work out the lessons we learned. Lesson three pertaining to self love would enact itself as I stood my ground with clarity to her about who I am and that I couldn't just break up to make up. That type of relationship served me no purpose as I needed to be around people who were constantly growing and forgiving while staying committed to each other and themselves. We came to an understanding and decided to give it one more shot as we really loved one another and saw much potential in our relationship. Yet one detail I learned during that time should have been the biggest red flag for me to understand the battle I was fighting from her past. Her father was a DJ in his young life and her father and mother's relationship ended due to his young and fast lifestyle as a DJ.

Again as I have come into my own journey at different stages I am reminded that trauma is passed down. Not only are we moving through our own sources of pain in life, our ancestors had issues and sources of pain that if they weren't able to conquer before us, we are bound to repeat the cycle. Our relationship pressed on for another year. We made it through a military deployment, post-deployment life, an intertwining of lives, possible engagement and the beginning of a world pandemic. Her family's past mixed with our present had a hold on her to believe even though her eyes and heart told her we were okay and could make it, her disbelief and trauma told her that we couldn't. My coping with trauma by shutting down when backed in a corner resurfaced and depression from military, work and life's trauma set in. We both needed help. Yet we continued to cope in our own ways which led to our unfortunate end.

A profound truth in life is that love and relationships are a mirror. They show us who we are and what we need to work on. Boyfriend or girlfriend, husband or wife, brother or sister, mother or Father. We are all reflections of one another. Since that last relationship I have received extensive counseling to understand my past and where I went wrong in all these relationships; including the one with myself. My own shortcomings, negative self-talk, lack of understanding who I am and what love truly is are in my daily perspective. I changed how I ate entirely by incorporating a more plant based diet and lost over forty seven pounds in two months with about an eighty percent diet change and twenty percent fitness. That opened up more mental and spiritual space and clarity for me to dig deeper and do more inner work. Incorporating yoga, deep breathing and meditation into my life have utterly changed my way of being and have opened me to more understanding about the world in which we live than I could have ever imagined. As I continue to grow and become one with my surroundings I am reminded that to be Ten Toes Down in love means to first love yourself. For we cannot love the being next to us if we don't first understand how to love the one we are with daily, ourselves.

"To consciously experience your own love is both therapeutic and liberating. Self-love heals the deepest wounds and removes the most abrasive insecurities. Self-Love liberates and releases us from the grips of painstaking memories of past hurt, failure, and traumatic experiences. Your love is a portal into you. To enter this portal, grants you access to all versions of you and provides you the power to heal the past and everyone in it. Self-love is soul medicine. To love yourself is to bring harmony and heaven to the heart."
- Londrelle – "Eternal Sunshine" 'Self-Love'

" ...to be Ten Toes
Down in love means
to first love
yourself. For we
cannot love the
being next to us if
we dont first
understand how to
love the one we are
with daily,
ourselves."

LARRY LOVE

12

DATING IN DUVAL

"Who does the hard thing? Those who are
willing, those who are worthy."
—Ebony Payne English – Colossus (feat. Markeyta) – Kuongoza Album

EUGENE "TREY" FORD III

DEDICATION

In loving memory of Lin Shell and DJ Terrah, and DJ OnQ.

Decide – to come to a resolution in the MIND as a result of consideration.

Using the word's origin, Latin, we can make it even simpler. Decidere is comprised of "De" which means "off" and "caedere" which means "cut". Thus, to decide is to cut off all of the other options. Burn the boats as they say. If you're unfamiliar with this phrase it comes from the story of Hernan Cortes and his conquest of Mexico. In order to prevent his military from considering a retreat he ordered the boats to be burned so their only option was to press into victory by any means necessary, a victory through which the spoils could provide for new ships among other treasures.

Being "Ten Toes Down" is a decision, or a string of decisions in a consistent direction. The defining moment is in that space of choice where you can elect to go in one direction or the other. The defining moment is when you actually TAKE ACTION in the direction of your decision.

So, what do you do when you know the "right" decision, the purposeful one, but want to shy away from it? What do you do with that lingering "thing" that you know you should be doing but have built up excuses, tools of incompetence used to build monuments of nothingness; posed as "logical reasons" not to do the hard thing? The hard thing that requires you to lift out of your comfort zone and embark on the path less chosen.

You cut off the retreat. Let the journey begin, there is no turning back!

LaQuinta by Wyndham NW Austin -Room 109
Monday August 9th 6:00am

(Alarm Blaring After Being Snoozed Twice) – *I guess I may as well wake up too,* I thought. My roommate from our IgKnight The King - "Lover immersion," Sway, a celebrity barber from Los Angeles by way of Mexico, had to wake up earlier than I did to allot for a twenty minute Uber to the airport. In April, I returned home immediately after the King immersion but this time I chose not to dive back into the regular hustle and bustle in Jacksonville right away. I wanted time to integrate and process everything we went through during those three days straight of twelve hour sessions. Not quite group therapy, not quite group coaching, not quite a "retreat" or at least not what we tend to think of when people mention they went to a retreat. The simplest way to describe it is a three day baptism in an "Iron Sharpens Iron" container developed specifically for men who can sense "the call".

The foundation of the IgKnight The King program is based around guiding men toward the sacred versions of our four archetypes: **The Lover, The Warrior, The Magician, and The King** as described in the book *"Rediscovering The Archetypes Of The Mature Masculine"* by Robert Moore and Douglas Gillette. The brotherhood thrives through pure transparency and firm but loving accountability.

During the immersions, each themed toward one of the four archetypes, we do everything from addressing past traumas to conditioning our minds and bodies for physical altercations, for war. The full spectrum of humanity expressed through men ranging from their mid twenties to early fifties. This is a group of men dedicated to doing the work necessary to show up in this broken culture and fallen society as the empowered masculine and not what has been dubbed "toxic masculinity".

We don't have any more time to waste with the direction and pace that society is going. Our world operates in a culture destined for stagnation with the systems of supremacy based in unbalanced patriarchy and the greediest versions of capitalism. Earth's most intelligent inhabitants are headed toward total energy neutrality, a world of docile horses destined for the glue factory to borrow the metaphor from George Orwell's *Animal Farm*. We are literally in The Matrix right now. One of my old sales managers used to always say, "You're either green and growing or brown and dying, there is no in-between."

In April of 2021 I attended the King immersion. It gave me the spark I needed to progress in multiple areas of my life including completing *Ten Toes Down vol.1 – The Mindset for Greatness* with six other authors. That book launched on 6/17/2021, (James Weldon Johnson's birthday). While becoming a published author and helping others do so is a great feat, it wasn't the only commitment I made. I left that immersion with a personal assignment, to use my voice and face to inspire a shift in mentality and activity.

My target audience is the black community, and my goal is to catalyze synchronicity amongst entrepreneurs, especially in the entertainment industry starting in Jacksonville and extending throughout the African Diaspora. The gap between the "haves" and "have nots" is widening and statistically there are more black people in the "have nots" section. Yet we have been distracted with conflict among ourselves, which has slowed down the pace at which we can establish footholds of wealth and resources. Crabs in a bucket, competing in every way possible instead of collaborating, and it has to stop ASAP.

I attempted to amend my assignment so it could be completed in a more comfortable manner, writing a paragraph about it in my chapter of the book instead of speaking on it. Life and death are in the power of the tongue, not the keyboard. If one were to attempt to amend the instructions on an assignment in school, they should most likely expect to receive a failing grade. We should expect the same when we shy away from our callings in life, and when we do so the byproduct is worse than an "F". We miss our destiny and rob the future of a gift we were purposed to deliver. I read a quote that defined hell as meeting the person you could have become and seeing the things you could have done, if only you had answered the call. My fear was that answering the call would make me a target for scrutiny, or worse considering the fate of many black men before me who walked that path.

Flashback - The Cookbook Restaurant after the "Life Outside The Game" Book launch
Sunday August 1st 3:00pm

I got my ticket to Austin, TX as a birthday gift from my friend Savita Jones, the owner of Alka Vita Alkaline Water and The Water Bar by Alka Vita. She has a unique concept that's a combination of a co-working space, intimate event venue, and beverage company offering smoothies, teas, water refreshers, and other drinks developed primarily by minorities. She paid for my plane ticket without hesitation during a planning meeting for an upcoming festival after I expressed that I may not attend the immersion because I couldn't find an affordably priced ticket #TenToesDown. Even though we haven't known each other for what would be considered a long time, there is a common "love" we share. Love is the answer that solves all problems, however many people don't understand that there are four types of love.

Eros is the one that is over sensationalized in today's society, sensual or romantic love. **Storge** is a familial love. **Philia** is a brotherly/sisterly love, hence why Philadelphia is called the city of brotherly love. I'm surprised a city up north is nicknamed the city of brotherly love, maybe it was different at the time of its naming. **Agape** love which is unconditional love usually used to describe God's love for humanity. Our love falls in the philia category especially because we aggravate the shit out of each other but get right back to working together once we get over whatever one of us did to annoy the other.

Savita and I met prior to me moving back to Jacksonville, Fl. She sponsored bottled alkaline water for the comedians and staff during the Fake Famous Comedy Tour's Jacksonville show April 6th 2019. At that time she was three years into the venture as the only black owned bottled water company in Florida, and one of few in the nation. My co-founder of Gainesville Black Wall Street, Aaron Daye, and I took a special interest in this product and the story behind it. Our initial objective was to create additional distribution channels in Gainesville where I still lived until August of 2019.

At that time Savita was running the operation out of her house near Franklin Arms with her business partner, fourteen years young, Mekhi (her son). And there was another heir to the "Water Queendom" on the way, Sareya, as Savita was seven months pregnant. Being in business while raising a teenage son, with a daughter on the way was challenging enough, but she was also on crutches with a broken ankle to boot (pun intended)! Ankle broken in four places, in a leg cast. We need to step our game up, I thought to myself. #BlackGirlMagic.

At Gainesville Black Wall Street we were "marketing tailors". Every business expansion and marketing strategy was designed custom based on the needs and areas of opportunity of the business. Instead of bringing a resume of our past work, we brought our Wealth Dynamics Profiles which described WHO we were by our gifts and strengths as opposed to a resume which describes WHAT one has done. I am a 'Star' profile, and Aaron, a 'Creator' profile. If you imagine the profiles arranged as a clock, Aaron would be positioned at twelve o'clock and as a Creator he sets the stage. I would be positioned at two o'clock and use said stage in the role of a master of ceremonies, shining my light and edifying the upcoming act. For a more in depth description of the eight profiles in the Wealth Dynamics Assessment search YouTube or schedule a call via **www.calendly.com/treyford.**

We developed a brand ambassador strategy and recruited strong figures in the Gainesville area to promote the brand including Pascale Belony who was preparing for the Miss Haiti pageant, my frat brother Eric Ramos who had survived a head on collision on a motorcycle November of 2017 to turn around and start a nonprofit that supports children with various programs throughout the year, Candace & Candace the mother-daughter duo who own Elegant Couture Boutique which had a suite in Hairport, an upscale salon on 34th Blvd. and several others.

Additionally we landed a few cases of water in Able Pharmacy, the only black owned pharmacy in town located on the NW side of Gainesville. When you consistently sow seed in good ground and do right by people, you always have a harvest when you need it. When you have platonic friends of the opposite sex you too can catch flights, not feelings. Stop trying to fuck your female friends fellas, Eros isn't for everybody. I'm telling you because I need to practice what I preach as well.

Downtown Austin
Monday August 9th 9:00am

I decided on a one-way trip so I could travel either to Dallas, Houston, or both while in Texas and fly back from the final destination. If you are unaware, Texas is massive! I thought both Dallas and Houston would fit into this trip, with the assumption that one city might be a stop on the way to the other. Needless to say, it was time for me to start looking more deeply at maps because I came to find out, Austin is about three and a half hours southwest of Dallas and roughly the same distance "west-west" of Houston. Houston is positioned about the same distance south east of Dallas, forming a triangle between the three cities. By Sunday August 8th with the help of my friend Britt who would also be my "Airbnb" for the week, I found an inexpensive bus that travelled from Austin to Dallas.

One of the reasons I decided to stay in Texas a few extra days was my propensity to people please and give more access than I should. Sometimes blind optimism causes me to take on more projects than I can truly handle well. In

Jacksonville there's a notion that the community only supports the popular or the people who are born and raised in the city, so I took it upon myself to disprove that, starting with my own efforts. That initiative sometimes puts me in multiple places throughout a sixteen hour-day, often including an event or project of my own. Being out of town was an easy pathway to saying, "can't make it," with a valid reason other than not wanting to. "I don't want to," is as valid a reason as any yet, being a natural servant and quite frankly one who also likes to be served (sow what you want to reap), I sometimes find myself saying yes to things I really don't feel like doing, begrudging the decision later or defaulting on my commitment.

In my chapter "Crash & Burn" from the previous volume of Ten Toes Down, I expressed the pitfalls of this especially when habitual. It remains something I need to work on. When it comes to men, this can create a dangerous pendulum, swinging between "weakling push-over" and "belligerent brute" once fed up with being used and taken advantage of. Only to return to weakling when the damage was done and regret set in from acting out in a way that came off much more volatile in comparison to the specific frustration at hand. Don't let that build up, in order to be Ten Toes Down for anyone else it must start with self-love and self-respect which is expressed through the self-discipline of saying "no" when you need or want to. Say no, boldly without remorse or any guilt around it. I caught a Lyft from my hotel into downtown Austin. I've been to Austin a few times but never truly experienced the city, typically traveling from the airport to the outskirts and back. This bus stop was my first chance to see downtown which wasn't much different than Jacksonville's downtown on a Monday morning. Homeless people congregated in specific areas strategic to finding shelter and asking for resources, the mixture of graffiti covered buildings with newly renovated ones, once vibrant and booming businesses now closed most likely due to COVID-19, with "FOR LEASE" signs in the window.

Downtown Dallas
Monday August 9th 1:00pm

Britt pulls up in a black Infiniti G37. *Ok Ms. High Value Woman!* I thought to myself. Kevin Samuels won't have anything to say about her economic status or dress size, if he ever decided to let her stream into his show that is. I found out while writing this chapter that she has commented and tried several times but he (seemingly) "don't want no smoke" with Britt.

Britt is originally from St. Louis, Missouri. She says "over hurr" and "thurr" like Nelly. She is thirty two years old, lighter complexion, about 5'5, athletic build but more on the slender side. She does contract work in therapy for government entities and has some budding ideas around what she can do in a private practice or entrepreneurial venture. In her trunk was a pair of roller skates, no doubt where her lovely legs come from. In her back seat there was a car seat for her fur baby, Benji, a seven year-old Pomeranian. I hadn't seen her since she came to Jacksonville to visit a friend and was looking for the right places to vibe with the right people in Duval County. Back in late 2019 we met through a Groupme chat called "The Wave", an entity that hosts several group chats categorized by city with the purpose of helping young black people connect and be informed about what types of events are going on any given day. "The Power Strip" is what I will nick-name this phenomena because all of the city's socialites, artists, plugs, and promoters had a captive audience. These micro-groups exist on WhatsApp, Facebook, and other social media platforms as well.

GroupMe doesn't get the credit it deserves as a networking tool and hell, dare I say, dating app? Founded in 2010, and acquired a year later by Microsoft through Skype Technologies, by 2013 it had over twelve million registered users sending well over five hundred million messages a month. I've been in several groups on the app which, for twenty five to forty five-year-old adults, has been used for everything from sharing investment ideas to airline price glitches and coordinating group travel to communication between volunteers on a church serve team or service organization. But primarily, it seems, it is used to find a worthy suitor.

Beto & Son at Trinity Groves
Monday August 9th 2:15pm

After a brief tour of Dallas en route to some food we decided on a Mexican restaurant, Beto & Son, that makes a dope frozen margarita with liquid nitrogen (Check it out with this link: https://bit.ly/betoson). From our conversation over lunch, dating in Dallas has a very similar narrative to dating in Duval. It helped me better realize the challenges going on between men and women, specifically black men and women, aren't hyper localized to my city but quite possibly a national or even global problem. I honestly don't even remember how we got on the subject, was this a date? What I do remember is how intrigued she was with the reason for my visit to Austin. "Black men don't do the work necessary to heal," she expressed. As a mental health professional and someone who would be considered an elite dating prospect, I valued her perspective.

On Biz Levin's Mango Season album there is a song called "Suddenly," that starts with this quote -".If lyrics on records could produce the kinds of negative results that certain people claim they produce then take this example. Most of the records which are broadcast on the radio are songs about love, 99% is about love, and all we hear on the radio is love…" - Frank Zappa interview on Larry King Live (1989).

Our ear gates and eye gates are constantly exposed to the topic of love which I believe has created a collective obsession. In no way am I trying to knock romance, but a huge area of opportunity for the black community to create more unity is increasing the value we have in STRICTLY platonic friendships, philia love. In strictly platonic relationships we can be more focused on reciprocal exchanges of energy, information, and resources sans the pressure of romance and presence of lust.

Racial solidarity order of operations – Step 1, end the competition between black men and black women. Step 2, end the division between rich or middle class black people and poor or working class black people. In a society haunted by race, being both middle class and black poses a special set of dilemmas. Over the past decades more black people have moved into the ranks of the middle class, highlighting the class differences that lurk just between the surface of African American life. Class is an uncomfortable topic for all

Americans and it is especially uncomfortable for black people. Minorities in America who have been oppressed never want to be perceived as oppressive. Somehow attaining success has become synonymous with losing your roots. Poor or working class African Americans believe middle class or rich black people are like white people and call them "uppity". A common slur is pointing out that someone grew up like the Huxtables which can even be seen in the Cosby Show spinoff, *A Different World* about Denise Huxtable, played by Lisa Bonet, going off to Hillman College.

However, some elitist complexes do exist amongst the black middle class and they tend to want to be set apart from black people from the hood or still living in the hood. They're dismissive and patronizing of people with less formal education than them. They start exclusive clubs that almost mirror the types of establishments black people were denied due to the color of their skin. Their Caucasian friends validate this behavior with microaggressions like, "You're so different from the other black people."

Another reason I am highlighting socioeconomic status is that the subject consistently rears its head in dialogue pertaining to dating. It starts with the conversation around how bills are allocated, beginning with paying for dates in the early stages of courting and extending into cohabitation or "shacking up" on the way to the marriage stage. We are in a whirlwind of change from the reformatting of gender roles, to the rise in high income earning women, to the decrease of backbone existing in men, all lending to more options and increased independence for women. Although statistically (and unfairly) women earn less than men for the same job, I have observed black women with better jobs altogether than their black male significant other, not to mention the women who are successful entrepreneurs. I personally don't know any women who **do not** want to be taken care of financially, and have security and luxury but the kicker is, they can do that for themselves now so they aren't about to put up with the bullshit their mothers and grandmothers put up with. Kevin Samuels has a video on YouTube titled "*Do Modern Women and High Value Men 'Mix'*" which I honestly haven't watched but the answer is yes, so long as he is not emotionally and morally bankrupt. Think about the type of man one would have to be to be married to a Proverbs 31 woman. (Read Proverbs 31 even if you do not believe the bible or identify as Christian).

How have our dominating thoughts and actions in life come to revolve around finding a romantic partner instead of finding ourselves? What can men do to bridge the gap in self care and mental health awareness?

Anyone who has been around me for a while has heard me say, "There are no such things as coincidences." It's called divine timing and alignment, being in the right place at the right time. It can even happen when scrolling through Facebook in spite of the algorithms. On August 9th after all of this talk about love and relationships I saw a post from a gentleman named Reylius. We did not know each other well but met each other a couple times around town, enough so to have become Facebook friends.

During my binge scrolling I come across a flyer with the red "CANCELLED" stamp on it that reads: "Higher Self: Men's Healing Group" on the top and the subtitle read: "Mental health, Financial wealth, Social well being. It was scheduled for Sunday August 15th from three pm to six pm. What made it interesting was he posted this on August 7th but I didn't see it until August 9th when I was about to cancel Culture Lounge for that week so I could stay in Dallas longer. His words above the flyer said: "Sooo this happened (frown emoji) I'm glad there's a few other spaces in this city for men on their healing journey. Travel well by brothers (Two hands emoji, fist emoji, fist emoji)

I commented below the post. "How do you feel about doing it on Thursday the 12th at Culture Lounge Jax? (7pm to 10ish).

His response: "Let's do it!"

Britt's Infiniti G37
Wednesday August 11th 12:43pm

While driving through Euless, Texas after dropping Britt off to a hair appointment, I get a text from Tiffy in a group message with her friend, a beginner DJ named Somayina. Our First Thursdays crew for Culture Lounge.

Tiffy: "Going forward, will you confirm with us before the Culture Lounge lineup for the month is released, please?"

Me 12:44p: Definitely. I'm under the impression that Karaoke + Game Night is every 1st Thursday so if ya'll ever need a "guest host" let me know but DJ MoneySis did let me know she won't be there for September. Are you going to be out of town too?"

Tiffy 1:07pm: "I'll be in town. It's a courtesy."

At this point I have a blank stare. I'm definitely appreciative of my growth over the last few years because I think my "Twitter Fingers" would have been activated with a different response than the one that followed. I hit the "Love" reaction on the text and listened to another song. Give yourself space to respond appropriately and always be curious before you are critical.

Me 1:11pm : "Cool let's just knock it out on the front end. October 7th, November 4th, December 2nd, I'm planning on releasing the October schedule in the next day or two so that's the only one I'll "need" confirmation on but those are the rest of the 'First Thursdays.'" The quotations around need was my subtle way of saying "get the fuck outta here" talking about courtesy when we already established a monthly schedule.

This was an eerie exchange. I sensed it spelled the beginning of the end of their tenured night at the Culture Lounge. I decided to call Chris Slade, the owner of Flying Write, who wrote chapter 8 in this book.

Chris answers: "Yooooooo."

Me: "Whattup man, Ima get straight to the point, we are probably going to need to make a pivot on First Thursdays. I'm pretty sure Tiffany and DJ SoMoney are about to be done on Karaoke + Game Night."

Chris: "What?! Why? Don't tell me it's cause she got a new boyfriend dawg."

Me: "Haha possibly, they are doing 'Game + Karaoke Night' now on Fridays or Saturdays at B&SUN Art Gallery. But this is basically what we set out to do. Most of the people who have hosted something at Culture Lounge have their own night somewhere else now."

Chris: "That's true."

We call Culture Lounge Jacksonville "A Process of Collective Enrichment" because the events curated there typically bring someone into new knowledge, or at bare minimum offers a new experience. But another reason we use that phrase is because my partners, Chris Slade and Brandon Byers, and I designed it to be an incubator of fresh concepts in the event planning industry. The goal was to add or activate event curating talent into the huge canvas of Jacksonville, Florida and beyond. Our "First Thursday's" curators of Karaoke + Game Night, Tiffany and Somayina, were ready to fly out of the nest with their own venues and event concepts, one of the first of which was a Thursday happy hour scheduled for August 12th at restaurant and lounge called Escape located in the five points section of Riverside. I missed their last event at Culture Lounge as I was flying into Austin that day, August 5th.

When people elect to move on and expand their reach the improper response is to be resentful or spiteful and we see it all too often. I wanted to be the opposite of that, proud and supportive so I set a reminder to stop by to say hello and grab a few videos to let people know it was going on, especially since Culture Lounge scheduled for that night was specifically geared towards men.

I can't act like I wasn't disappointed in their decision to move on. I totally understood though. We were charging five dollars a head for that night and splitting the profits four ways. With a venue the size of The Cookbook we could max out around two hundred dollars for the night, roughly fifty per person so only enough to cover any of the drinks or food we purchased at or after Culture Lounge.

In June, Tiffany and DJ So Money started doing Game & Karaoke Night with a venue owner named Leo from Chicago at his Afro-centric art gallery on Myrtle Ave near the Durkeeville area. The location is much larger than The Cookbook with positive messages painted directly on the walls which also housed African masks, artifacts, artwork, and photography all highlighting the beauty of intellectual blackness. My favorite photos are the mug shots of Martin Luther King, Tupac Shakur, and Malcom X. When you first walk in, to the right you go through an additional doorway where a stage is directly in front of you perfect for performance style events. Head left and up a few steps to the back of the room which has a kitchen to the right. The space is large so Leo invested in large black fans and positioned them throughout the rooms to assist the air conditioning in this humid Florida climate. Out the back door and down a ramp it opens up into a huge backyard space with a concrete block wall painted with the same themes of the interior of the building. This is where the smokers and talkers congregated but could still hear what was going on inside via an outdoor speaker adjacent to the ramp.

The venue has massive potential and I hope they max it out. Follow **@bsunbsun** **@tiffysimone** and **@djaysomoney__** on instagram to stay abreast of what they have going on there.

Britt's Balcony
Wednesday August 11th 8:25pm

I finally booked the return flight for Jacksonville.

Britt and I were talking on her balcony overlooking the pool in her complex. "Welp, at this time one of the two of us must vacate the balcony. My IgKnight The King weekly call is about to start"

"Oh, I can't watch too? I want to see what y'all talk about?"

"Absolutely not, men only," I said with a slight smirk. What is it about the ladies that they want to be a fly on the wall in these settings? I certainly have no interest in being in the audience for a woman centered event but maybe I should. She reluctantly obliged. "After the call is over, are you trying to watch a movie?"

While women like Britt embraced and encouraged the fact there were men actively pursuing strategies for optimal mental health, there were others who were very sarcastic and passive aggressive about a "Men Only" event. They acted like we were starting the "Big" Rascals version of the He-Man Women Hating club, and even if we were, we all remember how that ended. A coed group that was working in tandem, but it started from women and men meeting separately. Men need space to be with other men absent from the presence of women.

The men started the call sharing some of the wins and losses experienced between the end of the immersion which ended Sunday and that Wednesday. Oftentimes when people attend a conference or growth based event of any kind, by the time two or three days has passed the hype and motivation has worn off and individuals return to their conditioned patterns. Hearing some of the things the men shared validated my decision to stay in Texas and not return home right away. But even being at Britt's house there was a potential for me to backslide on some of the intentions I set over the weekend. I declared three vices I felt were robbing me of my full potential, **weed**, **women**, and **whiskey**. The Three W's. And when you are setting intentions, here comes a defining moment on the way to determine your commitment level. What action step are you going to take to advance forward?

Michael Diamond: "Would anyone else like to chime in and share something you want us to hold you accountable to as we enter into our season of the Warrior."

Me: "I'm committed to being celibate for the rest of August" I couldn't even believe the words as they were coming out of my mouth. In fact, I was almost watching myself say it on the zoom as a third party. Hearing, watching, and saying all at once.

Britt's Balcony During IgKnight The King Zoom Wednesday August 11th 8:44pm

Text from Jermaine: "Hey would you be interested in moderating the Q&A part of the Hip Hop Film Festival screening of "*I Had To Change*" representing Black Films Matter tomorrow (August 12th).

Text back: "I would, what time would the moderating piece start?"

Reply from Jermaine: "They asked us to log in at 9pm EST for a tech check but moderating won't start until after the film screens at about 11:00pm."

Text back: "Aiight, bet"

Jermaine J. Williams is an activist, author, artist, and now independent filmmaker who released his first project *"I Had to Change'"* this year, a documentary about him overcoming addiction. He's originally from P-Cola (Pensacola, FL) but currently resides in Jacksonville. Above average height but not super tall, thin build, low cut hair with a beard containing the texture mix of long and wiry with coarse and curly. A radiant smile sometimes including 6 golds to the bottom, Florida shit. In his face and eyes, you can see the trial and triumph simultaneously, the look of a war-worn warrior prepared for the next battle. And that battle takes place every day as he advocates and serves the youth in his hometown as well as Jacksonville, Fl. I remember once inviting him to an event that he couldn't attend because he was driving to Pensacola to organize conversations and next steps surrounding the tragic death of a high school football player to gun violence. The war for our communities is ongoing, and the fight is on multiple fronts.

We initially "met" through Instagram, most likely due to being in the same industry in the same place, the algorithms were kind to us to allow us to cross paths. Come to find out, we had a mutual friend in town, Krystal who also authored a chapter in this book, as well as my line brother (GOMAB) Jon Demps who was a football phenom that got a scholarship to University of Florida to play defensive end back in 2005. The worst part about Jermaine is his love for Florida State University, Go Gators!

I said yes knowing me moderating in between Culture Lounge Jax and the other stops I intended to make was going to be a tight squeeze. I immediately called my business partner, Aaron Daye, to see if he could fill in for me if I couldn't make it. Typically when it comes to Black Films Matter projects Aaron stays behind the scenes, putting me in the front and center as the face or the voice, somewhere I have been attempting to retreat from unsuccessfully thus far. *Answer the call.*

Britt's Apartment - Living Room
Wednesday August 11th - 10:07pm

After the zoom call I packed up my laptop and headed inside from the balcony. Britt was already on the couch, waiting to find out what movie to watch.

"Have you seen Judas and The Black Messiah yet? I didn't really get to watch it when we screened it earlier this year in Jacksonville."

"No, I haven't seen it yet. Honestly I don't know if I can handle it after the way Queen and Slim ended. I just don't see the point in setting myself up to be sad or angry, I gotta protect my mental."

"Overstood, I still think you should see it. As traumatic as the ending is, it makes up for that trauma with inspiration, plus this is historical."

"You sure it ain't nothing else we can watch?"

I pushed once more and she finally reluctantly agreed. I logged into my HBO Max account.

Before we started the movie I noticed a few bottles by the refrigerator. Watermelon Vodka by some company I'd never heard of. "What's this?" I asked.

"I have no idea, I think somebody gave it to me or left it over here one day. You can have some and pour me a shot too please."

Don't mind if I do, I thought. Maybe I can just replace whiskey with a different type of alcohol. I poured the shots and brought them to the sectional and we started the movie.

"What is the party line in regards to our sister's comrade?" Fred Hampton, played by Daniel Kaluuya, asked William O'Neal, played by Lakeith Stanfield, as he was attempting to flirt or holla at one of the ladies in the room during a meeting. "Uh..." William O'Neil smacks his teeth, stalling as if he was trying to locate the answer in an itemized file cabinet in his brain. "Anybody?" Fred Hampton prodded. "Do not take liberties with women" another panther replied.

By this scene we had been watching the movie for about fifteen to twenty minutes and took a couple more shots, but for some reason hearing this dialogue alerted me to how close Britt and I were sitting on the couch. It was like inception because I hadn't had any previous thoughts about "taking liberties". Why did he even say it like that? Can we 'exchange' liberties? What are the liberties?

"Get your mind out of the gutter Trey," I thought to myself. I looked at her and she must have seen my head turn in her peripheral vision because she turned as well and we locked eyes. I smiled, she smiled back, we turned back toward the movie. Twenty minutes later the same fella asking about 'party lines in regards to sisters' has a post sex scene with Deborah Johnson, the soon to be mother of his child.

Maybe I can start the celibacy thing after I get back to Jacksonville. The validation of withdrawing commitment process commences as my willpower to resist temptation continues to diminish. Britt gets more comfortable on the sectional and lays in the other direction so she can put her feet up...on my lap. I'm definitely not a foot fetish dude but, they were nice feet. Where should I put my hands with her laying like this? It was too much! I wonder what she's thinking about. Should I chance another look in that direction?

I risk a peek. This girl was knocked out. "Britt, you falling asleep haha, we can watch the rest tomorrow or something. I'm about to go to bed too".

"Nooo I literally just closed my eyes for a second.".

"You ain't got ta lie Craiiig," I joked.

We both burst out laughing.

"Why don't we just finish it in my room cause it's cold in hurr and I have more pillows in thurr."

Here was the first test. The defining moment, and I knew the longer I contemplated it the more likely I would fall. But I was already "seeing" someone in Jacksonville, and even though I'm single-ish I would have to let her know if something went down. She is just inviting me to finish the movie in a more comfortable setting, right? She stood up.

"Come on." she said.

"It's ok, I'm sleepy too so I probably wouldn't even make it but five minutes," I lied.

I was wide awake and ready for whatever. I remembered this quote that helped me with anxiety during standardized tests and move more quickly through them without overthinking things, "Study LONG, study WRONG," which to me translated as trust your instincts and act decisively.

I know beyond the shadow of doubt that had I gone into that bedroom I would have made some type of attempt or caught some type of hint. One of two outcomes, she obliged and within hours of making a commitment I would have broken it. Detrimental because every time you quit or break a promise to yourself it gets easier to do it. The second outcome could have been rejection. That would've been awkward the rest of my stay because I misread the signs and was tipsy on damn watermelon vodka of all things. Either way, round one goes to me, now for a cold shower in the guest bathroom.

Britt's Apartment - Guest Room
Thursday August 12th 11:00am

Text from Bri: Hey u up? I'm gonna set my alarm for 35 mins and wake up so we can get to the airport.
11:40am text back: Good Morning, sounds good.
Text from Britt; Good Morning! My bed feels SOOO GOOD (laughing emoji).
Hmmm, I bet... I almost found out last night, I thought. Daily action required, king, overcome temptation.

12:22pm Text to Coach Mechelle: I know I said I could do the live show this Thursday but I will be getting off the plane right before it starts., I guess that could be interesting for the audience?"
"Yes it will! Let's go ahead and keep it for today. I'll start the call so just hop on when you are able to."
"That'll work."

I started to pack up my things. I'm the type to wear pajamas on the plane but since my flight was going to touch down right before the Higher Self: King's Healing Circle I put on what I would be wearing to the Culture Lounge. Which reminded me to make a post to clarify the audience we were looking for tonight if it wasn't clear already based on the flyer.

"Tonight's Culture Lounge Jacksonville is for MEN ONLY".

The first comment that came was an associate who I know was being sarcastic but also has expressed disappointment in the dating prospects in Jacksonville. "Booo. I was going to come today too." I dismissed the comment with a chuckle as she has been to about 1 or 2 Culture Lounge events EVER. "Are we still on for Aromas on Sunday?"

"I think but let me make sure it's not for 'men only'."

"Sexism!" - another petty betty proclaimed. Somehow this joshing snowballed into multiple comment jabs including a GIF of Beyonce performing, *"WHO RUN THE WORLD, GIRLS!"* Not the response I was expecting from women who seemed to be starving and thirsting for men to be doing work like this so that they could qualify as better dating or marriage prospects. Even within sarcasm there is truth. "Men need to heal, go get therapy," was a daily post by the new social media relationship "expert" (who happens to be single, but because of everyone else not their own shortcomings of course lol).

I decided I would play along. I wrote a new status to bait them.

"Who Run The World. Girls? Hehe. Aiight BET #EmpoweredMasculine"

This post flew off the hinges with all kinds of debate and banter between men and women, too much to include in the chapter but if interested in following the dialogue you can check the post by typing the following link in your web browser: **bit.ly/girlsrunit**

TRIGGERED. The Battle of the Sexes

Jacksonville International Airport
Thursday August 12th 6:30pm

The flight landed a little bit early. The most exciting thing about this was knowing I would be able to take my mask off soon (COVID SUCKS). Showtime with Coach Get U 2Gether (Mehelle) is in fifteen minutes but I was sitting toward the back of the plane so I had to wait for each row ahead of me to grab their carry-on and mosey down the aisle. Once I got off the plane, I strategically pulled out a bottle of water as my reason for letting my mask hang to one side. Now to coordinate my pick up while simultaneously preparing to be unavailable on my phone. Timing is everything, especially in airport pick-ups because the people empowered to keep traffic flowing in the airport departures and arrivals lanes don't play.

Once I got situated I plugged in to the Facebook live:
5:15 – Coach Mechelle: "How important is it for us in this season of our lives to have someone who holds us accountable?"

Me: "It's paramount, specifically with men because the world is crying out for men to stand up in a big way right now. The buzz word is toxic masculinity but there is empowered masculinity that exists as well and it's necessary...But accountability across the board (everyone), we lie to ourselves so we need somebody (we can trust) to show us our blind spots."

Coach Mechelle: "…That is so true, my dad used to say if you ain't truthful with nobody else you definitely need to be true to you."

Me: "How can you be truthful with anybody else if youre lying to yourself?"

We talked a little further on that subject and I told Coach Mechelle I was headed to Reylius's "King Healing Circle" taking place at Culture Lounge Jax.

Coach Mechelle: "… A men's healing event, that is so vital because there aren't enough spaces that are created intentionally for men to heal… Intentional spaces created for (and by) men to heal amongst men, there are always things created for women because that's what we do, we are social, we'll get together, we'll cry together…"

Me interrupting sarcastically: "Y'all are social?"

Coach Mechelle: "Haha, yes we are, well I'll say my circle is."

Me chuckling: "All of y'all are social." (or at least more naturally than men in in this regard)

Whilst walking out to find my ride my service cut out. One of my co-authors from the first volume of *Ten Toes Down*, Shaqkena, was my ride from the airport. I let her use my car while I was out of town because hers was being repaired. In the **#TenToesDown** network we are growing, we see each other's needs and meet them without requiring the person to ask. Their needs are my needs, and vice versa.

Back on Facebook live at the 14:30 mark.

Coach Mechelle: "So tell us about Culture Lounge and your event for tonight."

Me: "Well tonight is actually not 'my' event. With the Culture Lounge I'm typically not the person who is curating the event, I'm creating the container except for when it's #Unplugged (live music), and we got Biz Levin – Unplugged coming up August 26th, that's mine but umm most of the tie somebody else is (hosting) the event so for example our hostesses for First Thursday's, Tiffany and Somayina, they're moving on as they started another Game & Karaoke night and are doing some other things. Their last one is September and we have a new Karaoke + Game Night host coming in October… So this Thursday it is Reylius' and we had another perfect fit to co-host, Rickey Dancy and Dante Jennings who created The Playlist Works podcast which is another circle for men's healing. They utilize music in their therapy and self-help. You have to guard your ear-gates and eye-gates, most music is about love and so there's an over infatuation with love and relationships and sex and things like that because that's all we are listening to."

We continued on this thread for a little while. It was really important for me to be riding instead of driving at this time because it enabled me to be fully present with the conversation. Teamwork makes the dreamwork and I definitely needed a drive on my team to scale up. Being present allowed me to internally confess that I still haven't fully pressed into completing this "I Have A Dream" speech assignment.

20:20 mark of the interview:

Me: "…There's something else I would like to address… there's a pandemic going on in the black community that has nothing to do with a coronavirus, it has to do with division… there are a whole lot of dichotomies in our community – Black Women vs Black Men, the masculine vs the feminine, Black Muslims vs Black Israelites vs The

'Energy" people vs the Crystal's folks... there are a lot of schisms and we are so distracted with each other that everyone else is running circles around us..."

Coach Mechelle: "You brought up a valuable point, there is way too much competition... It starts real small and it starts to spread and become bigger than it even originally was."

Me: "That sounds like a VIRUS! Do we need a vaccine for that? Where is Pfizer when you need em? Modera?"

Coach Mechelle: "Yes! We need a vaccine (that delivers) self-awareness and self-security because when we are secure in who we are, there is no competition, because there is no one like you. When we don't value (ourselves) we cannot value others."

Me: "It reminds me of something a local poet, Jody, said at the Black Films Matter private screening of Judas & The Black Messiah, and I'm paraphrasing here but it was something like when we think we are 'The Prize' in a competitive way it causes us to forget that other people are precious."

26:13 Me: "I mentioned a whole bunch of competitions between people but the number one competition we need to address is the competition between black women and black men... I'm not going to pretend to be the poster child for this because I've had issues with it as well and have failed and can grow in this area, so I just want to say to everybody, let's grow together... I don't want to 'go-together' (date), but let's grow together."

Coach Mechelle: "You know it would take five to six shows to even scratch the surface of this and I've done research on some of the root causes to the division between men and women in the black community but what I'll say is this, personal roles are more important than gender roles and acknowledging those helps us to not feel inferior or superior." You can catch the full conversation at **bit.ly/GetU2gether**.

By this time I'd dropped off Shaqkena and started making my way toward The Cookbook Restaurant. She let me know the last time she tried to get gas that the gas door wouldn't open but she sent money via Cash App so that I could fill up the tank. I looked at the miles to empty indicator, twenty two miles that should be enough to make this stop, slide to Escape on the way home and make it back to The Cookbook. I'll stop at the station later, I thought.

The Cookbook Restaurant
Thursday August 12th 7:10pm

Pulling up on Pearl Street I saw the parking lot was packed. All men ready for the King's Healing Circle which is atypical at a Culture Lounge event. When I walked into The Cookbook the fellas were shooting dice. I chuckled, and thought "Classic."

Inside were a mixture of men I knew and didn't know. Of the men I knew, were Mal Jones and DJ Tha. Chief even though they had to get to the Justice Pub for Lyricist Live – Uncut within the hour. My barber Jeff McCall, one of my closest high school homies, John E. Kennedy III, the battle rap and poetry king Moses West. Men ranging from their twenties to their fifties all were in attendance. Single men, married men, separated men, polyamorous men, the entire gambit. Divine timing and divine partnerships aligned to make this event ten times larger than the previous one according to a gentleman who had gone to the last healing circle. I passed a document called "*The Hero's Journey*" out to the men. It's an outline of twelve stages that men go through in cycles during their time on Earth. Then I hopped on the mic and edified the facilitators for the night, Reylius and Dante. Once they took the floor I walked out to hit my next destination.

When I pulled up to the five points area on Park Rd I could see DJ So Money bopping through the window smiling from ear to ear. "Woooooo," I could hear her on the mic muffled through the walls and my car window. Seeing someone thoroughly enjoy doing what they are passionate about always makes me happy. And her audience was jamming per usual. I found a parking spot and walked in and got a hug from Tiffy and fist bumped DJ So Money as she was focused on making her transition. All love. "Hey y'all just passing through, had to pick something up from the house and this was on the way." And as quickly as I had entered I was gone and on the way to Baymeadows Rd.

Got home, unpacked, and noticed a package. Something told me to open it before I left. JACKPOT! My mom had purchased two copies of "Rediscovering The Archetypes Of The Mature Masculine", for my birthday. I forgot I had asked but my mom is an educator and buying books as gifts is her specialty, much to my cousins' chagrin but to my delight. I grabbed them and opened my desk drawer to get a pen and sign them to give to Dante and Reylius for holding down this space for men.

Underneath the pens in the drawer I saw something I hadn't worn in forever. "That's where this has been all this time?" I wondered. I grabbed it and put it in my pocket. On the way out of the door I noticed the *Ten Toes Down* balloon table decoration I ordered from Sweet Events By Candy (Candace

Wallace) for vending at the Natural Beauty Fest Jax a couple weeks prior. It was still fully inflated and in good shape, so I grabbed it because I wanted to display it while vending at the end of our event. I also figured Charli, who wrote chapter six of *Ten Toes Down vol.1,* was somewhere vending downtown. I can give the display to her after we are done at The Cookbook, I thought.

I pulled back into The Cookbook parking lot at the perfect time because Brian White was just arriving and I needed help carrying some things back in. But also perfect timing because he brought 1 extra cigar and it was mine now. I don't usually smoke cigars but during the last night of our Lover Immersion in Austin, Jonathan Schmitz shared some of his favorite cigars with the brotherhood in celebration of a productive weekend. I decided when the night was over I was going to fire one up to put a seal on a successful night empowering men.

Toward the end of the night I decided to stand and share from the heart, "Men I have enjoyed hearing you all share transparently and be willing to be held accountable. Your work is my work and I have been able to glean from all of the experiences I was fortunate enough to hear about even with my being in and out throughout the night." I reached in my pocket and pulled out my wedding band. "Not a lot of people know this, especially in Jacksonville but I've been married since 2012, but when we got separated, at some point I took the ring off so it wouldn't need to be a topic of discussion when meeting new people. But that is misleading and dishonest, and I am sure there are even men who do it that are still actively with their wives, living with their families. So today, I've decided to get back in integrity with what ACTUALLY is, and put this ring on. I don't expect to rekindle the flame with my estranged, but I am making a commitment to staying celibate for the rest of August."

The response was a mixture of shock, applause, and proud nods of approval, but the comment that stood out to me was, "There is keeping it one hunnid, and there is keeping it one THOUSAND. That right there was a thousand man, damn, I salute you." I challenge everyone to be **H.O.T.**! Honest, Open, and Transparent is a place of total freedom and control. "The TRUTH shall set you FREE".

The bible says in 2 Corinthians 12:9-10 "'…My grace is sufficient for you, for my power is made perfect in weakness.' Therefore I will boast all the more gladly about my weaknesses, so that Christ's power may rest on me. That is why, for Christ's sake, I delight in weaknesses, in insults, in hardships, in persecutions, in difficulties. For when I am weak, then I am strong."

We started to wrap things up and say our goodbyes. I sold a few books and left the Culture Lounge to head to 1904 where The Cypher by DJ Monsta was taking place, and Charli was vending. "I have just enough time to drop the balloons and find a quiet place for Hip Hop Film Fest New York," I thought.

There wasn't a real (full) parking space available because of the way some asshole parallel parked so I parked on the corner half way into a handicap spot. I was just running in and out but I was down to thirteen or so miles til empty and those numbers can be deceiving so I decided to cut the car off. By the time I got back and tried to crank it up, it wouldn't start.

"Damn, I'm outta gas," I thought. I ran back into 1904 to see if anyone had a gas can. Seven Soul Jones said he didn't have one but he could give me a ride. "Ok bet, I'm going to ask around and if I can't find anyone with one I'll come back not urgent right now." As I walked toward the Justice Pub I thought, since it's the Hip Hop Film Festival maybe it would be dope to go live from the Lyricist Live. I tried in a few spaces inside and out but couldn't get the lighting right inside, it was Hot AF (as fuck for those unfamiliar with todays abbreviated ebonics) outside with the Florida humidity, and it was too loud anyway, but I needed to stay on the feed because Jermaine's film was going to end any minute now and it was up to me to start the moderating first based on the run through we'd had earlier that night. I lucked out and saw Tiffy headed to her car, she must have come by after their event at Escape. "Hey, in need of a favor, I think my car ran out of gas. Can you swing me by the gas station?"

"Sure hop in!" she said, and off we went to the first gas station and we started the post screening show in her car. At the first gas station we stopped, the inside was closed and only the pumps were operational. Tried the next closest gas station, same fate, *are gas stations closed after midnight in downtown Jacksonville or something?*

Running out of ideas with the inconvenience I was causing starting to wear on my conscience I told Tiffany it was ok and I needed to finish the live up stationary. I hopped out of the car, ironically in front of the Florida Theater. What a perfect place to wrap it up. Hopefully the guests watching the post show interview were entertained with all of the running around I was doing. Fortunately, Aaron went ahead and joined us on the stream, as well as one of Jermaine's crew members from the film.

When we were all wrapped up, the founder of the festival, CR Capers, joined on the line. "Ms CR Capers when are we going to get back going with the BLIMS (black SIMS). "Wait, who is this? Is this the same Trey from Clubhouse?" (laughter from all of us).

"Yes it is!"

During the pandemic when Clubhouse was first getting started, a collective of film industry folks started looking into different software for virtual campuses so we could continue to thrive even in a pandemic world. A small world at that. CR gave us all some nuggets on potential next steps and we joked about how open Florida was in comparison to New York before we logged off.

When we got off the facebook live Jermaine called me, "Where you at man?! I'm about to come scoop you."

When he arrived we went ahead and researched which gas station would have the store open and ended up going north of downtown all the way past MLK to grab the gas can. We talked about the trajectory of his film and all the doors the Harlem Film House was opening up for him. His film was the epitome of H.O.T., honest, open, and transparent, revealing things that most people take to their graves. That's why it was doing so well in all of the festivals it entered. It's the type of work that facilitates transformation in others.

After all of this running around I finally made it back to my Pathfinder. Fortunately it was still there with no ticket. I open up the gas door, secure the nozzle, and pour. Jermaine yelled out of the window, -alright man, you good?"

"Yes sir!" I responded.

I replaced the cap over the gas can, placed it in the trunk, and hopped in the driver seat. Foot on the brake, push to start… nothing. I tried again, this time after jamming the gas a couple times. Still nothing. Sigh… Maybe it just needs a jump.

At this point all I can do is laugh. These are character building moments where you need to slow down and smell the roses. Take a breath. I hopped out of the car again and headed toward Justice Pub. When I got there only Mal and Tha.Chief remained.

"Either of yall got jumper cables?" I asked.

"Yea I got some, they're in my car, it's parked in the alley. Just grab them, it should be unlocked cause I've been bringing my stuff out there."

I walked out to his car, grabbed the cables and started my trek back to 1904. Fortunately as I walked up I saw DJ Monsta Da Poet letting someone out of his passenger side right next to my car. "You got time to give me a jump real quick?" I inquired.

"Of course!" he responded. We clamp the cables onto the batteries, I hop on the driver side, foot on the brake, push to start, 'Vroooom'.

I sighed with relief. "Thank ya sir!" I exclaimed. We unhooked the cables for return to **@Tha.Chief** and I went south over the Main St Bridge headed to I-95.

What a night.

Aromas Cigar Lounge
Friday August 13th 1:25am

I pulled into the Aromas parking lot. One would think I had the type of night that would cause me to go straight home and get some rest. But I wanted to put a button on the night with a celebration in solitude. No whiskey-ginger tonight, I ordered soda water with a lime and pulled out the cigar from Mr. Brian

White. The bartender gave me a matchbox and after a few puffs to get it lit, I contemplated the week I'd had while people-watching, one of my favorite pastimes.

And then I thought of a looming defining moment for me.

"How am I going to tell her, '**No more sex**?''"

Proverbs 31:3
"Do not give your strength to women, nor your ways to that which destroys kings."
- The words of King Lemuel's mother, to her son.

"*I challenge everyone to be H.O.T.! Honest, Open, and Transparent is a place of total freedom and control. "The TRUTH shall set you FREE"*

EUGENE "TREY" FORD

Meet The Authors

Tierra Simone Edwards

Tierra Simone Edwards was born in Charleston, South Carolina, but she calls Norcross, Georgia home where she grew up. She was born on the 2nd of March and is a true Pisces at heart! Tierra's biggest accomplishments are graduating from LeCordon Bleu with an A.S. Culinary Arts Degree and publishing her first guided journal entitled "Spoonful of Purpose ". In her spare time Tierra loves to be out in nature, write, read, dance, sing , and inspire others to live like they are Born for Purpose! One of Tierra's core foundational beliefs is "Being present in every single moment granted, because every moment gives us something to take with us to our next level." Tierra is also the creator of Born4Purpose Inc., whose mission is to plant seeds of purpose into the hearts of girls and women.

Tierra aspires to continue writing and publishing in the future, become a life coach for teens and young women, and establish Born4Purpose Inc as a movement that lives in the hearts of girls and women.

Contact Info:
www.bornforpurpose.com
Email: live@bornforpurpose.com
IG: _bornforpurpose

Destiny Whitehead

Destiny Whitehead was born in Portsmouth, Virginia and raised in Washington State. She resides in Jacksonville, Florida where she started a full-service bartending company called Mr.Barrtenderr. Although she has a background in finance and wealth Management however, her passion was creating cocktails and playing a mad scientist with spirits. She gained momentum by conducting Cocktail Creation Classes for small groups during the Covid-19 pandemic shutdown in 2020/2021 and partnered with Culture Lounge to make the experience bigger and greater. This led her to an opportunity to work privately with spirit owners of color to showcase signature cocktails that she created with their brands. She is an experienced instructor with a small bartending school based in Jacksonville, Florida where you can learn anything from cocktail waitressing, obtaining Bartending Certification, to marketing for bartending and anything in between.

For more information and to connect with Destiny visit:
www.mrbarrtenderr.com
Instagram: @Mr.Barrtenderr
Email: mrbarrtenderr@gmail.com

Shevonica M. Howell

Shevonica M. Howell is the mother of Andre V. Caldwell, II and Te'Rana Aliyah Austin. Her grandkids are Audre' Renae Caldwell and Andre Vincent Caldwell, IV. She is a decorated Army veteran, published author, motivational speaker, and the founder and Chief Executive Officer of Academy of Scholars, Inc. Ms. Howell recently accepted two more titles as the Literacy Coach of JaxPAL and a Guest Services Supervisor with Safe Management. Ms. Howell faithfully attends Friendship Primitive Baptist Church, she is a mentor to many, and she believes in spending quality time with her family. Ms. Howell's favorite pastime is promoting her books and her school, but what she loves more than anything is giving testimony!

MORE BOOKS BY THIS AUTHOR

Girl, they Ain't ready!/ I CAN DIG IT SIS ... THEY AIN'T READY!/ What's in a Name? Stop Making Excuses ... SHIT HAPPENS!/ A Play with Words Word Search Puzzle Book/ The"YOU TEACH IT" Math Study Guide/We Love You, Dre!/A is for ... Audre'/ Te'Rana Aliyah A BEAUTY WITH BRAINS/Finding Myself ... Am I Enough?/Hi, I'm Jada! Hello! We are Jarrod & Jeremiah ...

Contact info:
https://www.facebook.com/shevonicam.howell
Twitter: Shevonica M Howell
Instagram: @shevonicamhowell
ShevonicaMHowell@gmail.com
(904) 274-1107

Aaron Daye

Aaron Daye was born in Durham, NC, and currently resides in Gainesville, FL where he serves as the Chief Photographer for the University of Florida Foundation, co-founder of Black Films Matter and owner of Daye in the Life Media which combines his photography and graphic design companies Gorillaz Ink and Aaron Daye Photography. He is an award-winning photographer who has been published in over 50 publications including the New York Times, Sports Illustrated, Ebony, Women's Day and the Florida Gator Alumni Magazines. Aaron holds a bachelor's in visual communications from North Carolina Central University and uses his talents and skills developing branding for community organizations and small businesses. Aaron continues to make his impact on the Gainesville community through his involvement with several community organizations such as the President of the University of Florida Association of Black Alumni - Gainesville Chapter, a Founding Board & charter member of 100 Black Men of Greater Florida GNV, Inc., and a member of Alpha Phi Alpha Fraternity, Incorporated.

For more information and to connect with Aaron visit:
https://linktr.ee/aarondaye
Instagram: @aarondayephoto | @GorillazInk |
@blackfilmsmatter
Email: aarondaye@gmail.com

Arnisha T. Johnson

Arnisha T. Johnson was born and raised in Jacksonville, Florida, graduate of Douglas Anderson School of the Arts, alumna of Converse University, and currently a Certified Law of Attraction Life Coach, Business Performance Strategy Consultant, and CEO of Manifesting On More, LLC. She has coached and consulted over 20 MomPreneurs within the first 4 months of operating her business, helping them grow their mindsets and businesses. With her degree, certification, experience, passion, and expertise, Arnisha serves MomPreneurs by helping them with their mindset, their vision for their families, and their business, ensuring that every MomPreneur becomes the CEO of themselves, their family, and business. When Arnisha isn't coaching, she's spending uninterrupted time with her family, enjoying her Sabbath, and connecting with elevated, like-minded individuals. Although she doesn't reside in Jacksonville, FL anymore, about once a month, you can catch her in town.

For more information and to always stay connected, visit her
Website: www.ManifestingOnMore.com
Facebook personal page:
www.facebook.com/CoachArnishaTJohnson
Facebook business page:
www.facebook.com/ManifestingOnMore
Instagram: www.instagram.com/ManifestingOnMore
ClubHouse: @ManifestOnMore

Krystal R. V. Elzy

Krystal Renae Vivian Elzy was born in Biloxi, Ms. Moved to Pensacola, FL at the age of 3. Moved to Jacksonville, Fl in 2018. Currently holds a Bachelor's of Science degree in Human Resource Management. She enjoys self-care, finding new adventures and most of all spending time with her son. She is free spirited and lives her life to the fullest. She's ambitious and is driven to succeed in her own way.

For more information and to connect with Krystal visit:
Krystalelzy81@gmail.com
Instagram: miss_lz

Wadelene Charles

Wadelene Charles is a Holistic Wealth Accountant at Grand Reve Financial, Wealth Coach & Educator and Chief Financial Officer of IV Kings Investing Group. Wadelene obtained two Bachelor's degrees at the University of North Florida in Accounting and Finance and a Masters in Accounting at Keller Management alumni. She currently holds a 215 Life and Health Insurance License and has been in the Accounting & Finance field for over 12 years. Money is more than just part of the job description for her: it is a duty to her community. She strives to normalize financial literacy, educate her community about money and sustainable financial habits, and ultimately fortify the resources of future generations. Wealth Education is Wadelene's impact and legacy on the world. It's her way of helping to change the experiences of those around her. She enjoys gardening, spending time with family & friends, and writing poetry that she wishes to one day share with the world. She recently released her Tax Courses and working on releasing her first financial literacy book.

For more information and to contact Wadelene Charles visit: www.grandrevefinancial.com or Learntaxcourses.com
Instagram: @wadelenec @grandrevefinancial
Email: info@grandrevefinancial.com

Chris Slade

Who is Chris Slade? The name Slade is an acronym which stands for See Life And Do Everything. Chris explains, "That's how I want my life or career to be in the end. I want to be able to say I really did that. So my name reads Chris Saw Life And Did Everything." Slade is from Jacksonville, Florida and although he began pursuing a rap career years ago his journey has become so much more. As a rising educator, entrepreneur, curator, artist, activist, and now author Slade has much to do in order to secure his legacy, but he is more than up for the task. Follow him on his journey through marriage, new fatherhood, music and business, his album "READY", and just keeping his head above water in the steady grind of Jacksonville, Florida. Get READY.

Meet Chris Slade:
IG: @flyingwriteworld
www.ChrisSladeMusic.com

Simone a.k.a "Sage Reeds"

Simone or "Sage Reeds" was born in Lauderhill, FL, and she currently serves as the Editor-in-Chief of sagereeds.com and the Head of Writing at Sage Reeds Media. She is a copywriter, editor and newly certified writing coach with 10+ years of experience in the creative writing field. When she's not working to meet her clients' storytelling needs, she enjoys tending to her plant babies, reading, loving on her loved ones, napping on the beach and indulging in all things fashion and art. She is currently writing a full book titled, A Piece of Peace, which will serve as an extension to her Ten Toes Down chapter (chapter 9). A Piece of Peace will be released in 2022.

For more information and to contact Simone, visit sagereedsmedia.com.
Instagram: @sagereedsmedia
Email: sagereedsmedia@gmail.com

Manouchka "Sandie" Doreus

Manouchka Doreus was born in Miami, FL, and currently resides in Jacksonville, Fl. She is currently the owner of Torq LLC, a car rental company, and co-owner of Home Grown Property Solutions LLC, a real estate investment company. Manouchka currently holds a bachelor's in Psychology from University of North Florida and uses her training to write impactful, thought-stimulating poetry and spoken word. Manouchka uses her art to bring social awareness to depression, abuse and hopes to impact the world with deeply honest and uncomfortable conversations through her new Youtube series titled, "A Naked Conversation".

Larry Love

Larry Love was born in Jacksonville, FL and is currently the Founder and Creator of RnBMostly, LLC and Love Creates, LLC. He is a national DJ, Event Curator, Creative, Music Manager for the music collective L.O.V.E Culture and is himself an Artist. Having created and executed hundreds of events around the U.S., Love enjoys bringing people together for all types of occasions. Larry also served 9 years in the United States Air Force. When he is not working on his creativity to create his future, Larry enjoys spending time with his son, Seth. He also travels the world doing yoga and spiritual self-work while trying out exotic fruits and eating healthy foods. Love is currently working on his first Debut album titled "God of Louve", working on his future full book and prepping to become certified to become a Doula.

For more information and to connect with Love visit
Website: www.createinlove.com
Instagram: @iamdjlarrylove
Facebook: www.facebook.com/iamdjlarrylove
Email: larrylovecreates@gmail.com

Eugene "Trey" Ford III

Eugene Ford III, better known as "Trey" was born in Louisville, KY, but has spent most of his life in Florida between Miami, Gainesville, and Jacksonville, where he currently resides. He graduated from the University of Florida, where he pledged the World-Famous Zeta Kappa Chapter of Phi Beta Sigma Fraternity Incorporated while earning a degree in Agricultural Operations Management. He is the co-founder of Black Films Matter LLC, a film programming company that creates dynamic viewing experiences centered around black TV & Film. While in Jacksonville his goal is to create synergy through edutainment events that bring like-minded people together, allowing for organic collaborations to be conceived (Jacksonville Renaissance). An avid networker, movie-buff, new farmer, community organizer, adventurer and book worm, who loves helping people embark on new entrepreneurial endeavors. Most importantly, Trey is a #girldad with 2 lovely daughters, Savannah (7) and Layla (2).

Connect with Trey: www.calendly.com/treyford
IG: @treysolo7
FB: @TreyFordImpresario

Made in United States
North Haven, CT
10 October 2021

10249548R00164